12 REMARKABLE *Scots*

BOOKSTORE

This book is dedicated to Margaret,
for her unending patience,
encouragement, and love.

Contents

About the Author

JERRY'S first project as a writer was at the Edinburgh Fringe in 2001. Since then, he's written and produced a further two plays. In film he produced a short documentary and a short drama before turning to the printed word.

Jerry has spoken at many venues and events, including the Edinburgh International Book Festival, Glasgow's Aye Write Book Festival, the Mitchell Library, the Dick Institute in Kilmarnock, the Robert Burns Birthplace Museum and the National Library of Scotland and to many groups and societies.

More recently Jerry has spoken at the William Patrick Library, Kirkintilloch on the life of Beatrice Clugston, one of his *12 Remarkable Scots*.

Also by Jerry Brannigan, with John McShane and David Alexander: *Robert Burns in Edinburgh*, published by Waverley Books, ISBN 9781849341714.

> "It is both a most informative guidebook for the tourist to Edinburgh and an essential addition to the library of Burns enthusiasts, giving extensive details on all subjects and personalities that Burns may have encountered … I wager you will not be able to resist reading it from cover to cover at the first sitting."
>
> *Burns Chronicle* 2016

To nominate a future *Remarkable Scot*
please contact the author at jerry@jerrybrannigan.com

Introduction

AFTER completing my first book, I gave a lot of thought to the direction of my next project.

In our work with *Robert Burns in Edinburgh*, I was struck by the amazing, wonderful, remarkable Scots we stumbled upon as we put that book together. I wanted to continue this theme of researching and revealing the lives of people I didn't know much about at all.

But how to find my Remarkable Scots?

At a family wedding, Claire, my nephew's wife, asked me what I was working on. When I told her, she said she couldn't help: "How could I know anyone famous?" "I'm not looking for famous, I'm looking for interesting," I tried to explain. A few minutes later she returned with, "My great-uncle was a painter. He died when he fell off a wall in Italy when he was young." I knew that was the hook, but what was the story? After a little thought, she said, "I think he might have been one of the Glasgow Boys."

That definitely got my attention. In the end, she was close: not a Glasgow Boy, but a deserved first of my Remarkable Scots.

Emails to friends on various writers' groups brought a flood of suggestions. I felt it important to find as wide a variety of subjects as possible, from a variety of eras, and an equal balance of sexes. Some names I knew, some not, but all worthy of initial research.

Now, as we are about to publish, having spent so many months examining their lives, it has been very easy to become emotionally tied to every one of my six men and six women, each of whom have their own uniquely remarkable story.

In many cases, individuals or societies already champion their lives and achievements in an effort to introduce them to a wider audience. I have been very pleased to join that wider audience.

Finally, many thanks to Claire Cameron, who did know someone famous after all.

—Jerry

12 REMARKABLE *Scots*

Six men and six women
whose lives have touched
the history or culture
of Scotland

Alan Fletcher. Self-portrait. c.1956–58. Photographic reproduction in greyscale by
Jerry Brannigan. With permission of Hannah McCorkindale.
© Hannah McCorkindale.

Alan Fletcher

ALAN Fletcher was born Alan Robert Tregoning Williams Fletcher on 27th March 1930 at 8 Finnieston Street in Glasgow, the youngest child of Archibald Fletcher and Mary Williams, and a half-brother to Doris.[1]

Archibald trained as an engine fitter and worked as the boiler maintenance engineer in the Central Hotel in Glasgow, while Mary was a hotel manager in the Cornwall area. Born in Cornwall, it is thought Mary came from a line of Cornish Gypsies. The name Tregoning is of Cornish extraction, meaning 'homestead'.

With the complete redevelopment of the Finnieston area in the early 1950s, the family moved to a top-floor flat at 144 West Graham Street in the city, only a short walk from the Glasgow School of Art (GSA).

Pencil sketches found in his portfolio folder show that, even from a young age, Fletcher drew regularly. His pencil portraits suggested a talent yet to mature, a talent put on hold when, in his late teens, he developed rheumatic fever. In the 1940s, rheumatic fever was a common cause of heart disease in children and young adults. It had the potential to cause great and irreparable damage to heart valves and muscles. Fletcher was admitted to Oakbank Hospital in the city, a specialist centre for treatment, where he spent many months as a patient. Despite making a full recovery, the months spent in hospital and in recuperation disrupted his education to the extent he didn't complete secondary school until the age of 18.

Just a year later, Fletcher was declared fit to serve his country and to carry out the statutory 18 months' duty of National Service. Family discussions suggest he became a sergeant with the military police, and rumour has it he carried out work for the British Intelligence Service. Perhaps this experience led him to find a part-time job as an undercover operative in a Maryhill bakery in his home city of Glasgow. He was tasked with discovering how so much bread was finding its own way out the doors but, despite several letters from the management, Fletcher failed to submit any reports targeting his fellow workers. Eventually, he found himself sacked as the company's 'inside man', but, due to his likeable nature, and being skilful in his part of the bread-making process, he still kept his job.

Alasdair Gray, a contemporary and close friend of Fletcher's at the GSA, recalled that when Fletcher was recounting this story, he suggested to him that "... *he was embellishing or even imagining the story*". An indignant Fletcher was able to produce a box containing the letters from the bakery management, confirming his role as a failed spy![2]

Due to his hospital stay and National Service, it was September 1951 before Fletcher was admitted to the GSA; at the age of 21, a little older than the majority of students. Fletcher immersed himself in student life. With his friend, cartoonist John McGlashan, they became involved with student magazines *GUM* and *Ygorra*, developing their respective styles through their contributions. As a student, Fletcher drew some of the cover pages and illustrations for the annual Students' Day *Ygorra* magazines.

Carole Gibbons, fellow painter, said of Fletcher, "*On first sight he was very impressive, almost majestic, he had a long loping walk, like a white Ethiopian.*" The two, the cool and beautiful Gibbons and the hip and handsome Fletcher, were naturally drawn to each other and soon became partners, Gibbons moving in with Fletcher at the family home in West Graham Street. They were to spend almost all their time together and talked of plans for their future. The couple took a photograph of themselves on the steps of the GSA, which they termed their 'betrothal' picture.[3]

Alan Fletcher with figures. Glasgow School of Art. From the personal collection of Alasdair Gray. With permission of the Alasdair Gray Archive.
© Alasdair Gray Archive

13

Their closest friends were Douglas Abercrombie and Alasdair Gray. Gray had joined the GSA later than the others but immediately found in Fletcher someone he could look up to and admire. Fletcher was the older, more mature, dominant character of the group of painters who identified with his talent. "*Confident and wild,*" Gibbons called him. But, for all of this, he was genuinely interested in the work of other painters and enjoyed their companionship. They too wanted to be in his company because, as Gray put it, "*... being with him felt like going on an adventure*". These adventures were journeys in art. Fletcher constantly looked at ways to develop his painting and sculpting, forever keen to experiment and talk about his work. Gray said that in all his time at the GSA, he learned most from Alan Fletcher.

The adventures regularly continued long into the night at West Graham Street. Its proximity to the GSA meant it attracted many of his artist friends at the end of long days spent working on their own art. Hannah, Fletcher's niece, recalls the atmosphere. "*They would all be in the kitchen, talking, painting. Alan was always painting, he painted on anything he could find. Carole was always there, Alasdair Gray as well. Douglas Abercrombie, John McGlashan, lots of others. One time, Alasdair Gray painted a mural on the back wall of the bed recess where my Granda read. My Gran would go away to work in hotels and when she came back the place was redecorated!*" [4]

On one occasion, Hannah recalls being sent by Fletcher to the local butcher to collect a sheep's head. "*The butcher handed it to me, wrapped in newspaper, and I had to walk home with it, dripping blood everywhere. I think I remember every step back to the flat.*" A delighted Fletcher set about capturing the beast's bloody head on canvas. In 2001 Inverness Museum and Art Gallery received a Scottish Arts Council Bequest of Fletcher's work, *Sheep's Head*, painted in 1958.

Fletcher had a problem focusing on the basic elements required for the first two years of the general course, as he felt the time spent on this was an unwelcome distraction from his own painting and sculpting work. With timekeeping that was erratic at best, he was in danger of losing his place on the course.[5] Fletcher approached Benno Schotz, Head of Sculpture, and asked if he would accept him on the sculpting course. He explained he wanted to study under someone whose work he respected and in whom he had faith. Schotz knew of Fletcher's work, of his originality and potential, and had no reservations in accepting him on the course.

Schotz was so impressed with Fletcher's attitude in the studio, and the innovation in his work, that he made Fletcher his assistant in his private commissions. In some ways, it was a case of the student becoming the teacher. Schotz admits that Fletcher 'mechanised' him. Before Fletcher's arrival, he did all of his metalwork by hand, using hacksaws and files to work the metal. Fletcher insisted Schotz obtained an electric drill, saws, a grinder and an electric welder to ease his workload. They would work in Schotz's home studio, creating and planning the construction of larger pieces. Fletcher would then travel with Schotz to assemble the finished work in location.[6]

Schotz, writing in his autobiography, *Bronze is in my Blood,* wondered why Fletcher was late not only for classes at the GSA but, when working at his home, often didn't arrive until late morning. He found out later that after working all day at the GSA or Schotz's home in the evening, Fletcher would paint late into the night. In the morning, he would go to his local baths to swim and freshen up before heading to classes.

In the late 1950s, there was a general disquiet amongst students that their work was not being fairly represented, creating an atmosphere of resentment that the GSA management was doing little to create outlets to show their students' work. So frustrated were the students that in 1957, in an effort to have their work shown to the public, Fletcher and five other painters hung their work over the railings of the Botanic Gardens on Queen Margaret Drive at weekends. It was also felt that the Royal Scottish Academy had not moved on from the late 19th century, when even the Glasgow Boys, a group of painters known and revered throughout the art world, had to fight against the same acknowledged Edinburgh bias.

In the mid-1950s, three young painters, James Spence, Anda Paterson and James Morrison, formed the Glasgow Group, which also came to be known as the Young Glasgow Group. Inviting seven other students to join them, Fletcher replied with his acceptance: *"I must agree with you, the Institute is an insult this year and I have come to the conclusion that instead of trying to convert them the thing would be to build afresh with creations as a foundation."* Amongst Fletcher, Gibbons, Gray, Abercrombie, Knox, McAslan and McCulloch, the aims of the Young Glasgow Group were agreed. They would collaborate in staging exhibitions and, even though individually their work was of a very diverse nature, they realised that to succeed, they would have to work as a single entity to make their mark. However, as John Morrison concluded in his *Friday Event Lecture, Independent Art in Scotland in 1955–1965*, *"… no one doubts that Fletcher is the key"*.[7]

Fletcher was always outspoken in his support of the group. After an open-air exhibition planned for the Botanic Gardens in Glasgow was handed over to the Glasgow Institute, he was vocal in his condemnation. Once again, the students felt they would be subjected to the aged bureaucracy of the Institute, *"I'm afraid the open-air show, which had great possibilities in this respect, is becoming a kind of Institute in modern dress if you know what I mean …"*. It is little wonder that art from the West Coast of Scotland was looked on in many circles as stagnating.

In 1957, director Eddie McConnell produced a short film, *Observations on Life at the Glasgow School of Art, 1957*. Included are shots of the final year degree show. *Man on Wheel* sketches, *Lamp on Table,* and a terracotta head, *Mary,* all works by Fletcher, are clearly seen.[8]

Fletcher's course came to an end with the awarding of his Diploma

in Sculpture in 1957. Schotz commented, "*My belief in his quali-
ties was vindicated when he finally took his Diploma with great credit,
being awarded a travelling scholarship.*" Fletcher was granted the John
Keppie Travelling Scholarship and a special drawing prize awarded by
Sir William Hutchinson, RSA.

Shortly after Fletcher gained his diploma, Schotz was awarded a
commission for a new Catholic church, St Paul's, in Glenrothes. It
was the first church to break from a traditional rectangular layout,
and Schotz was commissioned to create the high altar cross. With a
very short deadline, Schotz and Fletcher worked on it day and night.
Alasdair Gray confirmed it was Fletcher who suggested making the
instruments of the passion, the nails, hammer, crown of thorns, etc.,
from welded iron. They worked together on the assembly, Schotz creating the figures and emblems, and Fletcher working on the cross.
Today, St Paul's remains one of Scotland's most important post-war
churches, and is a category A listed building.

Some months after being awarded the travelling scholarship, Fletcher decided to travel through Europe with close friend
Abercrombie. They visited Brussels and Berne before arriving in
Milan. Here, Fletcher met with a tragic accident the day following
their arrival. Reports vary on what may have happened. Surrounding
the hostel was a 4-foot wall, but only on the building side. On the
other, was a 20-foot drop. A local police report suggested that when
Fletcher woke early in the morning to find the hostel doors locked, he
most likely climbed out of his ground-floor bedroom window. Then,
not realising the drop, jumped over the wall. The hostel janitor found
Fletcher's lifeless body at the foot of the wall.[9]

Alan Fletcher died in the grounds of the Student House, 62 Viale
Romagna, Milan, on the 1st August 1958, aged 28.

The news was barely believable when the story broke in Scotland.
Hannah recalls arriving at her work to be shown the front page of the
newspapers and not being able to stop crying. At home, her brother

heard their mother letting out a most awful scream when she opened the newspaper. She collapsed in the street later in the morning. Her Gran and Grandad, Mary and Archie, "… *were totally distraught, they never got over it till the day they died*".

Carole Gibbons recalls how she couldn't take it in and, looking back, thinks she must have been in shock for weeks and months afterwards. "*I stayed on at West Graham Street, I didn't even think to move out. My mum and dad were ok with it and so was Alan's family.*"[10] For several years after Fletcher's death, Gibbons, Abercrombie and Gray visited Alan's parents at West Graham Street or, on occasion, dropped into the boiler room of the Central Hotel and spent time gossiping with Mr Fletcher.

Benno Schotz and his wife Milly were heartbroken at the news. When working at their home, Fletcher had meals with the pair. On one occasion, Schotz said to Fletcher, "*You are like a son to me.*" Fletcher riposted, "*And I'm like a father to you.*" When the Schotzes went to West Graham Street to pay their respects to Fletcher's parents, it was the first time Schotz had seen where Fletcher had lived and worked, writing that "*It was beyond my understanding …*" how Fletcher was able to paint in such a cluttered space, and yet he somehow managed to produce many fine paintings and sketches.[11]

Alasdair Gray was utterly devastated. He believed that, even as a student, Fletcher made paintings and sculpture that proved him an artistic genius. In his later books, he based several of his characters on Fletcher, saying, "*He was the free-est and most intelligent man I ever met, so a diminished version of him later appeared in three of my fictions. Had I not diminished him he would have stolen the attention from my main characters, versions of me.*"[12]

After Fletcher's death, the Foreign Office organised and paid for his funeral in Milan. By November, Fletcher's father, Archibald, began to receive letters from the Foreign Office requesting repayment of the funeral expenses and a further letter on 23rd January 1959, asking

Alan Fletcher

Man on Wheel
Alan Fletcher
c.1958
With permission of
the Alasdair Gray
Archive.
© Alasdair Gray
Archive

19

that he "*... reply immediately to the letters addressed to him*". Archibald replied, advising the Foreign Office that he was not in a position to make the payment, but he believed that there would soon be an exhibition of his son's work, which would allow him to settle the debt in July. The Foreign Office accepted this offer.[13]

In the meantime, Fletcher's friends realised, as the accident happened at the beginning of his tour, only half of the grant had been paid out and the GSA still held £50 in his account. Fletcher's mother, Mary, wrote to Director Mr Douglas Percy Bliss on 11th May asking that the GSA governors pay the funeral expenses (of £26:5:10d) and suggested the balance be used to buy materials to allow his friends to frame some of the work to be exhibited.

The GSA responded as Fletcher himself could have predicted. They called on solicitors and chartered accountants for advice, agreeing on 14th May that the funeral expenses could be paid directly to the Foreign Office. However, the question of funding the framing of Fletcher's work could not be put to the governors until confirmation came from the Arts Council that an exhibition would go ahead.

The Arts Council wrote to Director Bliss on the 27th May confirming that the memorial exhibition would take place 11–24th June in the McLellan Galleries, Sauchiehall Street, Glasgow, but to make it possible asked that the GSA release the final £24 of Fletcher's grant so his friends could frame and hang the pictures.

In his reply two days later to Mrs Kemp, Exhibition Officer of the Arts Council, Director Bliss intimated that he had "*no knowledge that Mr. Schotz had actually put forward the scheme to your Committee*" and, as the Board of Governors of the Glasgow School of Art would not meet until the 19th June, "*... I think you must accept the fact that there will be no assistance from the Arts Council in connection with the exhibition*".

Director Bliss ended his letter to with a PS: "*I assume that Mr. Schotz will be briefing the opener of the exhibition. It would be a great mistake if it was not clearly enough pointed out how generous the bursary authorities, and, indeed the School of Art, had been to this student. He had six years of studentship here, and it is no exaggeration to say that he gave us more trouble than any other student in my time. But we put up with this, in the hope that he would prove to have unusual abilities.* "[14]

This writer is of the opinion that Fletcher would have been delighted that, even in death, he still managed to irritate the GSA management.

However, it should be accepted that Director Bliss almost certainly wrote in frustration at the circumstances in which he found himself. Having no knowledge of ongoing discussions between Schotz and the Arts Council of a proposed memorial exhibition, Bliss must have felt it was reasonable for the Arts Council to provide the means for the framing the pictures.

Director Bliss could feel vindication that, despite the 'trouble' Fletcher had given him in his time at the GSA, within a very short period after his death, it was generally recognised that Alan Fletcher had indeed possessed 'unusual abilities'.

Alan Fletcher, 1930–1958: A Memorial Exhibition took place in the McLellan Galleries, opening on the 11th June 1959. In his introduction, Schotz wrote, "*Fletcher's paintings can now be seen as autobiographical and subjective. His self-portraits, and portraits of his friends, his lamps and ladder carriers, and above all, his, 'Man on Wheel', so precariously balanced, so tense and full of fear. Alan Fletcher had an inherent fear of accidents, and he made no secret of it, as if he had a premonition that one day fate would play a trick on him.*" He continued, "*His work was in the broad stream of the modern movement, and as we look on his paintings now, are left wondering what might not his future have been in terms of paint and invention.*"[15]

In August 1960, on the second anniversary of Fletcher's death, Alasdair Gray made the trip to Milan with Mary Williams, Fletcher's mother, to visit the spot where he was found and to see the headstone erected on her son's grave. Unfortunately, Fletcher's Christian name, Alan, had been misspelled as Allan.

In the immediate years after Fletcher's death, anxiety grew among family, and others, about the treatment of his work. Particularly as, in the two years before the Milan accident, he had been at his most prolific, completing many paintings and sculptures. Some of this work had been exhibited and sold, leading to disquiet in Fletcher's family, who had no knowledge of what was happening to the money from these sales or indeed where Fletcher's work was going.

Gibbons lived and worked in Spain between 1965 and 1967. The poet JF Hendry had become her patron, enabling her to travel to Menorca to focus on her painting. On her return to Glasgow, she wrote in a letter to Hendry, "*There's been a great stramash over Tony Armstrong's handling of Alan Fletcher's work*".[16]

In an effort to resolve the problem, Archibald Fletcher made Carole Gibbons the trustee of the whole of Fletcher's work and, with the assistance of Professor McLaren Young, the highly respected Richmond Professor of Fine Art at Glasgow University, a letter was drafted to Tony Armstrong. The letter alleges that Armstrong removed paintings from Glasgow University and that these paintings were sold at his gallery on St George's Road, Glasgow. The university confirmed in a letter to Archibald Fletcher on 12th February 1968 that they had purchased Fletcher's painting *Don Quixote* in September 1966 and were "*... very shocked to hear that you have still not received any payment from the Armstrong Gallery*".[17] Similarly, Dundee Art Gallery and Museum made three purchases of Fletcher paintings from the Armstrong Gallery. In 1968 a frustrated Gibbons, in a letter to Hendry, wrote that they (the Dundee Art Gallery and Museum), "*... despite my advice went ahead – the only thing I could then do was to insist that the money for the three for Dundee go direct to the Fletchers*". Gibbons continued, "*Tony has been owing them money for two years*".[18] It remains unclear if Archibald ever did receive payment for any of the paintings that were sold, or indeed the number of paintings that were involved. Carole Gibbons remains the trustee of Fletcher's paintings and sculptures.

Alasdair Gray never forgot Alan Fletcher. In his book, *A Life in Pictures*, he devotes a chapter to his friend, complete with a considerable number of images of Fletcher's work. He felt that, in a place where he was showcasing his own life's work, it was a respect he had to show to Fletcher's memory. Gray explained, "*I wanted to show as many pieces of Alan's work as possible, because no one else was going to do it.*" Oscar Marzaroli's photograph of Fletcher's portrait of Alasdair Gray, with the young Gray posing in front of it, was included in the Marzaroli exhibition at Street Level Photoworks in Glasgow in December 2019. (The exhibition closed due to the COVID-19 pandemic in March 2020 but opened again in September of the same year.) When a copy was sent to Gray by Malcolm Dixon, the gallery director, Gray was genuinely touched, immediately forwarding a copy to this writer. This exchange occurred only days before Alasdair Gray's death on 29th December 2019.

William Hardie, art historian and acknowledged authority on Scottish painting, wrote of Fletcher that his "... *premature death in an accident in Milan at the age of twenty-eight robbed Scottish painting of one of the most exciting young artists of his generation*".[19]

Hardie was the Keeper of Art for Dundee Art Galleries in the mid-60s, purchasing three Alan Fletcher paintings from the Armstrong Gallery in 1968 for the museum.

After his death in 2021, Hardie's art collection was sold at auction in Glasgow. His belief in the talent of Fletcher became apparent when two pieces, a painting, *Lamp, Still Life*, and a sculpture, *Underwater Hunter*, were included as part of his personal collection. Both sold over estimate at £1,500 and £3,500 respectively.

There is little doubt that Fletcher died on the cusp of an

extraordinary career. Only a few months before his death, the French Institute of Edinburgh's annual exhibition featured five young Scottish artists considered deserving of its recognition. They selected Fletcher alongside David Miche, Edward Gage, Elizabeth Blackadder and Frances Thwaites. A critique of the exhibition concludes that "*it is left to Alan Fletcher to fire off the exhibition's big guns*".[20]

In 1987 Alasdair Gray organised a touring exhibition, *5 Scottish Artists on Show*, displaying the work of Gibbons, John Connelly, Alasdair Taylor, Gray himself and, almost 30 years after his death, Fletcher. Gray included him because, as he wrote in the introduction, "*I believe that Scottish painting, especially in the Scottish middle west, would have been healthier, with more public growth had Alan lived.*"[21] Newspaper reviews of the show stated, "… *his six works stand out. They are flat, simple, austere still lifes and figures, verging towards abstraction with a perfectly judged use of subtle and limited range of colour in each*", and, "… *in him Scotland lost a powerful force in the art world*".[22]

Fletcher completed many fine pieces to great acclaim, having work exhibited in New York and Moscow, as well as many Scottish galleries. In the months prior to his death, his painting, *Sheep's Skull*, was displayed in the Royal Scottish Academy, while in the short period after his death, at least 14 pieces of his work had been purchased by public galleries and museums throughout Scotland. It was all work completed while he was a student.

In the course of researching Fletcher's story, two paintings, self-portraits executed while he was still at GSA were revealed to this writer. The paintings were handed down by Mary, Fletcher's mother, through the generations and kept in storage in cupboards for over 50 years. The paintings will be assessed for restoration.

There can be little doubt that had Alan Fletcher lived, he would have become a hugely influential figure in the world of Scottish art, and he is still missed by many.

Alan Fletcher
Self-portrait. c1958.
With the permission of the owner.
Photographic reproduction in greyscale by Jerry Brannigan.

Despite Gray's words written shortly after Fletcher's death, with the assertion that "*he will not occur to us much again*", Alasdair Gray never did forget Alan Fletcher.[23]

LAMENTING ALAN FLETCHER

He will not occur much to us again
unless in the thin way thoughts occur
who was wild and solid and broke doors in
and had women and clay his hands knew how to touch.

Now what we love in him deprives us of him.
Jokes, height, fox-grin, great irony and nose
will not occur much to us again.
They have been put in a box to rot.

Night air took the heat from his brain
As he lay cracked head under a wall.
Metal and stones stay shapeless because he is dead.
His clay crumbles. His women mate elsewhere.
He will not occur much to us again.

Alasdair Gray

Alan Fletcher Artwork in Exhibitions

Institut Français d'Écosse.
West Parliament Square, Edinburgh.
Five Young Scots Exhibition. February
1958.

123rd Annual Royal Scottish Academy
Show.
Edinburgh. 24th April 1958.

National Serigraph Society.
19th Annual Exhibition.
New York. May 1–29 1958.

The Inaugural Exhibition of the Young
Glasgow Group
McLellan Galleries, Glasgow. August
1958.

Alan Fletcher Memorial Exhibition.
McLellan Galleries, Glasgow. 1959.

Exhibition of Work by the Late Alan
Fletcher.
The Citizens Theatre Gallery. 27th
October 1963.

Scottish Council for Nuclear
Disarmament.
Exhibition of Paintings by Scottish
Artists.
McLellan Galleries, Glasgow. 1st March
1964.

The Five Artist Show, with Alan
Fletcher, Carole Gibbons, John
Connelly, Alasdair Taylor and Alasdair
Gray.
McLellan Gallery, Glasgow. December
1986.
Talbot Rice Gallery, Edinburgh.
January 1987.
The Municipal Gallery, Aberdeen.
February 1987.

Alan Fletcher Artwork in Public Institutions
Please contact the venue before visiting
Aberdeen Art Gallery & Museums

Two Pears on a Plate. 1958.
Purchased 1969. Accession No.
ABDAG002193.
Oil on Canvas. Ref. Art UK. 106957.

Man with a Ladder. c1958.
Scottish Arts Council Bequest, 1997.
Accession No. ABDAG013573.
Pen and Ink on Paper.

Drummer.
Scottish Arts Council Bequest, 1997.
Accession No. ABDAG013572.
Pen and Ink on Paper.

Glasgow Museums Resource Centre (GMRC)

Hill Street from George's Road, Glasgow. (recto) 1956.
Gift. 1989.
Accession No. PP.1989.57.
Ref. Art UK. 83975.

Study of an Art School Model (verso). 1956.
Gift. 1989.
Accession No. PP.1989.57 (verso)
Ref. Art UK. 83976.

The McManus: Dundee's Art Gallery and Museum

Lamp and Pear. 1957.
Featured in the As We See It: Twentieth Century Scottish Art 23rd February 2019.
Ref. Art UK. 92389.

Still Life with Lamp and Cup. 1957.
Purchased from the Armstrong Gallery, Glasgow, with the assistance of the National Fund for Acquisitions. 1968.
Accession No. 5-1968.
Ref. Art UK. 92388.

Young Girl (Girl with Red Hair). 1957.
Purchased from the Armstrong Gallery, Glasgow, with the assistance of the National Fund for Acquisitions. 1968.
Accession No. 4-1968.
Ref. Art UK. 92387.

Hunterian Art Gallery, University of Glasgow

Don Quixote.
Purchased from the Armstrong Gallery, Glasgow. 1966.
Accession No. GLAHA: 43494.
Ref. Art UK. 138479.

Divers on a Diving Board.
Sculpture c1957/58.
Accession No. GLAHA: 44369.
Purchased from Archibald, Mr & Mrs Fletcher (05/1968).

Man on Wheel.
Serigraph Print.
Purchased from the McLellan Galleries. 1959.
Accession No. GLAHA:18259.

Seated Nude.
Serigraph Print.
Purchased from the McLellan Galleries. 1959.
Reversed inscribed "by Alan Fletcher / No.113 in Memorial Exhibition Glasgow 1959"
Accession No. GLAHA:21339.

Alan Fletcher

High Life Highland Exhibition Unit

Sheep's Head. 1958.
Purchased 2001 Scottish Arts Council Collection Bequest, 2001.
Accession No. EU SAC.056.
Ref. Art UK. 165891.

University of Strathclyde, Glasgow

Lamp on a Table. 1989.
Gift from Alasdair Gray. 1989.
Accession No. GLAEX A389.
Ref. Art UK. 155749.

References

1   Conversation with Hannah and Ronnie McCorkindale. 20th February 2020.
2   Conversation with Alasdair Gray. 6th December 2017.
3   Conversation with Carole Gibbons. 23rd January 2018.
4   Conversation with Hannah McCorkindale. 20th February 2020.
5   *Glasgow School of Art* (GSA), Student card, Alan R. J. Fletcher. GSSA/REG/7/1.
6   Schotz, Benno, *Bronze is in my Blood* (Edinburgh, 1981). p. 212.
7   John Morrison. Glasgow School of Art Friday Event Lecture. 5th December 2008.
8   GSA, Observations of Life in the Glasgow School of Art, 1957. https://movingimage.nls.uk/film/3352
9   *Aberdeen Evening Express*, 2nd August 1958, p. 16. col. 2.
10 Conversation with Carole Gibbons. 23rd January 2018.
11 Schotz, Bronze is in My Blood, p. 212.
12 Gray, Alasdair, *A Life in Pictures* (Edinburgh, 2010). p. 45.
13 Glasgow School of Art Archive. (GSAA) DIR/12/1/13/15, Papers of Director Douglas Percy Bliss concerning Alan Fletcher.
14 GSSA. DIR/12/1/14/14, Papers of Director Douglas Percy Bliss concerning Alan Fletcher.
15 Benno Schotz. *Introduction to Alan Fletcher Memorial Exhibition*. McLellan Galleries Glasgow. June 1959.
16 University of Glasgow Special Collections. (UGSC) MS Gen 549/610.
17 Fletcher family archive. Letter. 12th February 1968.
18 UGSC. MS Gen 549/609.
19 Hardie, William, *Scottish Painting 1837 to the Present* (Glasgow, 2010). p. 179.
20 *Edinburgh Evening Dispatch*, 15th February 1958.
21 *The Five Artists Show,* Introduction. 1986.
22 *Press and Journal*, 9th February 1987, p. 10 col. 2.
23 Gray, Alasdair, *Between Whiles*. 1957–61. With permission of the Alasdair Gray Archive.

Victoria Drummond. With permission of Catherine Drummond-Herdman.
© Catherine Drummond-Herdman.

Victoria Drummond

VICTORIA Alexandrina Frances Drummond was born on 14th October 1894 at Megginch Castle, Errol, Perthshire, the second of four children to Captain Malcolm Drummond of Megginch, groom-in-waiting to Queen Victoria and his wife Hon. Geraldine Margaret Tyssen-Amherst. Captain Drummond's occupation is listed on Victoria's birth certificate as a 'landed proprietor'.

Victoria was a god-daughter of Queen Victoria, after whom she was named.

As a child, she often stayed with her maternal grandmother, who had an interest in woodworking and allowed Victoria to help operate her lathe. It was not entirely unusual in this family for the women to be independent,[1] as her paternal grandmother was a taxidermist and her mother a noted geologist.[2] Her younger sister Frances, a gifted artist, had a picture accepted by the Paris salon.[3]

Educated at home, and discovering an aptitude for mechanics from an early age, Drummond set her sights on becoming an engineer. As a young child, she was happiest loitering around the farm, watching blacksmiths at work or estate workers repair agricultural machinery. The engineering works of Robert Morton and Sons of Errol were near to her family home, allowing the young Drummond to be a frequent visitor, and enabled her to explore her interest in all things mechanical. It was Robert Morton who advised her she would have to serve an apprenticeship in her quest to become an engineer.[4]

In February 1913, Drummond discarded her overalls to change into her best coming-out gown when her parents took her to London, to the court of King George V and Queen Mary. A 200-year-old ritual, being presented as a debutant to the monarch, was followed by a busy season of events, dinners, and balls, all designed for debutants to show themselves to potential husbands. These prospective partners would, of course, be of the same upper-class society as their potential wives who, in effect, were announcing they were now 'out' and ready for marriage. Queen Elizabeth put an end to the practice in 1958 as the system was viewed as embarrassingly out of date in a modern post-war society.

The idea of a 'lady of society' becoming an engineer was looked upon as absurd in the first half of the 1900s but, far from being discouraging, her parents arranged for a teacher from Dundee Technical College to tutor Drummond in maths and engineering at home three times a week.[5]

She gained an apprenticeship at the Northern Garage in Perth from 1916–1918, where she worked on a variety of engines and vehicles, training under Mr Malcolm, previously a naval chief engineer. Malcolm taught Drummond one of her most important lessons: listening. He taught her to attune her ear to the various sounds of an engine; only by a detailed knowledge of the operation of machinery could she know instantly if something was going wrong. She would call on this skill for the rest of her working life, a skill which proved to be particularly useful in the middle of a hostile Atlantic.

Whilst Drummond was working on her apprenticeship, her sisters were working at home helping their mother with war work, organising local farmers to get their produce to shops and troops. They would also take the places of gardeners who had been called up. At least once a week, before she began her day at the garage, Drummond would rise early and make butter. When she finished working on engines, Drummond would help Jean and Frances pack apples for transit.[6]

In 1917, Jean left to work at the Gretna Munitions Factory. It was a vast project, so large that villages, which still exist, sprung up within the 9-mile-long site. At one time the numbers working on munitions exceeded 30,000. Drummond explained that Jean's job as a supervisor in the acid section, responsible for 200 women, was so dangerous that nothing metallic could be worn lest it reacted with the acids. The girls who worked in this section were known as 'canary girls' as it yellowed the hair and skin.

Today, on a small section of the original site, stands the Devil's Porridge Museum. The museum pays tribute to the many who worked here on the war effort, producing an explosive concoction which came to be known as 'The Devil's Porridge'.[7]

At the end of the war in 1918, Jean was struck down badly with Spanish Flu, an influenza pandemic which killed around a quarter of a million people in Britain.[8] When she was well enough, she returned to Megginch to recuperate. Several weeks later she returned to Gretna to finish her time there before moving to London in 1919 to take charge of the Queen Victoria Working Girls' Club, which was based in 122 Kennington Gardens. A little later Frances moved across the street to number 143, where she worked as a commercial artist.

When Drummond left the Northern Garage, she found another apprenticeship from 1918–1922 with the Caledon Shipbuilding & Engineering Company in Dundee, training as a pattern maker for metal casting, completing her apprenticeship in 1921. To celebrate, Drummond followed the long-established custom of 'paying off' from her first journeyman wage to 'stand treat' to her workmates. Drummond took 70 Caledon workers to a night's entertainment at the King's Theatre Music Hall, where she had reserved seats in the grand circle for two separate parties on different nights.[9] [10] There are also tales of Drummond holding a tea party at her family home for fellow apprentices because she could not take them to a pub. The society newspapers were to fill many column inches relating Drummond's life at sea throughout her career.

In 1922 Caledon suffered a shortage of orders, and Drummond, along with many other workers, was laid off.

From 1922 to 1924, Drummond found a post with the Blue Funnel Lines, joining the draughtsmanship department in Liverpool.

The subsequent interest from newspapers forced the company to, "... *emphatically deny that she was going to sea in any engineering capacity in a Blue Funnel boat*".[11]

Drummond joined the Blue Funnel Liner *Anchises* as tenth engineer, and completed a five-month round trip to Australia. In November 1922, while in Sydney, the Australasian Institute of Marine Engineers admitted Drummond as an honorary associate of Sydney District, and presented her with the Institute's emblem, "... *a beautiful gold brooch in the shape of a propellor, in recognition of the unique distinction of being the first marine engineer of the gentler sex*".[12]

On her return to Britain, there was much discussion about whether this was a suitable job for a woman. One of the engineers from the *Anchises* told the waiting press, "*At every port there were pressmen waiting to ask Miss Drummond how she liked it. But she was always adamant on the point of publicity*". The silence from Drummond, or of her employers, may have been influenced by the fact she sailed as an ordinary working engineer, as she could not sail as a certified marine engineer until she had 18 months' seagoing experience.[13]

The Imperial Merchant Service Guild contacted the Board of Trade suggesting that women were not legally eligible, to be told that due to the Sex Disqualification (Removal) Act of 1919, there was no reason why a qualified woman could not be employed.[14]

The district secretary of the Amalgamated Marine Workers' Union stated, "*The owners of the Blue Funnel Line allowed Miss Drummond to sail in the* Anchises *to enable her to complete her 18 months at sea and qualify to become a fully certified engineer, and there is not the least chance of their repeating the experiment. ... she is not likely to go to sea again*".[15]

In 1923 Drummond made the first of an eventual four journeys to Australia, with a final journey to China, leaving the company and returning home when her father died in 1924. With failing eyesight, he'd had a fall at Perth General Railway Station, slipping from the platform onto the rail, sustaining, among other injuries, a fracture to his right leg. Sadly, and to the great shock of the family, he died at Perth Royal Infirmary on 29th May.[16] While at home, Drummond used this time to study for her second engineers' exam, which she passed on the third attempt.

In October 1926, while working with the British India Line, she gained her Board of Trade Second Class Certificate (Steam) and, accompanied by her sister, visited Dundee Technical College to receive the certificate and the congratulations of all the staff and students who were eager to meet her. The certification allowed her to become the first woman member of the Institute of Marine Engineers. In the early part of the 20th century, as women were fighting for equality in many fields, her qualification as the first woman marine engineer was regarded as an event of outstanding importance and significance.[17]

Drummond then worked as fifth engineer on a trip to Africa, followed by four voyages to India before leaving the company in 1928 when work became scarce. During the depression of the 1930s, there was little demand for marine engineers, and none for a woman.

In this time, she continually studied for her chief engineer's certificate, taking the examination on 31 occasions, failing, or being failed, each time. Mr Martin, from Dundee Marine Engineering College, knowing Drummond's dedication and experience, continued to support her, and in 1936 tackled the examiners. Martin suggested to Drummond that they always failed her because she was female.[18]

Despite being accompanied by glowing references, all applications were rejected. Disappointed at being unable to find a position despite a shortage of engineers, Drummond, like her sisters, moved to Lambeth and lived with Frances. The absence of a job led them to begin a business breeding and selling tropical fish, something they had done at home in Scotland as a hobby. The business was a success, bringing the sisters many commissions.

In March 1938, after attending trade fairs in Leipzig and Prague,

Drummond and Frances travelled to a trade fair in Vienna. On crossing the border into Hungary, the atmosphere changed; German troops were guarding the bridges, lines and stations. In Vienna itself, crowds of youths wearing Nazi armlets marched in groups through the streets. Overnight, the hotel rooms filled with German soldiers. A British consulate official arrived to check on the girls' safety, confirming Hitler's advance troops had arrived in the city, and urging the sisters to leave the country while they could. As they had some time to wait on their train, Drummond decided, despite severe misgivings by hotel staff, that they would change into their best frocks and go to the opera. When Drummond decided to do something, a few German soldiers were not going to stop her.

The Vienna State Opera House was a self-contained world of opulence and grandeur. When the overture began, worries of the outside world disappeared. However, when the final curtain fell, they were given a *"... terrible awakening"*. From the top of the magnificent grand staircase, they looked down to find German soldiers everywhere; the stairway, the foyer, where a camp kitchen had been set up, every inch of space was packed with German troops. Swept downstairs with the departing crowds, the sisters found themselves surrounded by troops. The girls were rescued by the theatre manager who guided them back into the theatre, aiding their escape with the orchestra via the stage door.

Locked in their hotel room, the girls had a bird's-eye view of Hitler's arrival in the city. Standing in his limousine, acknowledging the crowds with his trademark salute, Drummond was able to take a photo of the German leader. *"I leaned out as far as I dared to take photographs, with Frances holding onto my legs"*, she explained on her return.

Their train was not due until 11.30pm, but, heeding the warning from the consulate, they arrived at the station well in advance of departure time. Fortunately, Austrian police, and not the German army, were checking tickets. Their British passports and passes for the trade fair allowed them to board the train, leaving many others crowding the barriers.

The attendant who accompanied the sisters to their adjoining sleepers, requested, in a hushed tone, if they would mind sharing one sleeper as the train was so crowded. He then asked for their passports, explaining that this meant they would not be disturbed at the frontier. When Drummond explained that they would be more comfortable keeping their own passports, the attendant explained in a whisper, that this was, *"a matter of life and death"*. The passports were handed over to him.

Much later, when the train came to a halt at a frontier, the girls could hear talk and whispering outside their door but could only decipher fragments. 'English ladies who do not want to be disturbed' seemed to be the general meaning. Gradually, the talking stopped as those in the passageway moved further down the train. The following morning, the attendant brought the sisters hot coffee and their passports. *"They thank you,"* he said as he left.[19]

It is thought that Jean was involved in facilitating the adoption of Hungarian children, and in some way Frances and Victoria were also involved. Rumours persist within the family that the real reason for the trip to Austria was to help Jewish friends escape the country before the German onslaught. It is suggested that, with the collusion of the conductor, the sisters may have achieved their goal on the last train out of the city. Sadly, it seems the truth about the trip went to the grave with Baroness Strange, Victoria's niece and biographer.[20]

In June 1938, the normally quiet and shy Drummond gave a talk at the *Conference of the Electrical Association for Women (EAW), at the Empire Exhibition in Glasgow,* on the effects of electricity on marine engineers. She spoke of the French liner *Normandie* and of the *Queen Mary*'s electrical system being big enough to light a town the size of Eastbourne. Her lecture, as a female engineer, was ground-breaking.[21]

When war broke out in September 1939, the three sisters volunteered for the Auxiliary Fire Service (AFS). Drummond, now 45, found that when not on duty at the air raid post, she could go to the Royal Albert Docks and personally approach numerous ships in her search for a post as a second engineer. Each enquiry met with no success. A chance meeting with members of a past crew led to an introduction with an agent for a foreign flagged ship. "*If the Red Duster won't have you, go foreign*", she was told. The 'Red Duster' is the nickname for the flag of the British Merchant Navy.

In May 1940, advancing German forces overran French forces in the north of France, driving British troops towards the English Channel and the only route to safety from Dunkirk. In the south, Italy was making headway against a depleted opposition, forcing stranded British citizens, and others, to scramble to find ships while ports were still open. From Dunkirk, all available ships in the area were used. From Cannes, two aging coal ships fled to Gibraltar, decks and holds filled with refugees. Some1,500 British subjects were evacuated before the port fell into Italian hands. An account of the last ship to leave Marseille tells of a rusting coal collier, the *Cydonia*, making sail for Gibraltar crammed with 800 British and French refugees. Both coal ships and the *Cydonia* made it safely to Gibraltar.

On the 19th March 1940, Drummond joined the SS *Har Zion* (Mount Zion), a small Palestinian owned ship working around the Mediterranean, as a second engineer. The SS *Har Zion*, played a significant part in the evacuation of Marseille, carrying one or both British consuls, escaping elements of the British Expeditionary Force (BEF) and as many refugees as they could carry. On her return, she was invited to a meeting of Lambeth Council where Drummond told councillors, "*I'm afraid I haven't done much. I brought back a cargo of rice. We were torpedoed once – a hair-raising experience, but one becomes convinced after a time that these Nazis are frightfully bad shots. But I am very proud to have helped in the evacuation of the B.E.F.*".[22]

The Atlantic was a perilous place for merchant seamen during the Second World War. Great Britain depended on imports to sustain the war effort, and relied on the Merchant Navy to maintain vital supplies from around the world. Victoria travelled many times across the Atlantic to Norfolk in America, Murmansk in the Soviet Union, and Halifax in Canada. To protect the ships, they were organised into convoys. This kept the ships together, with many having a mounted gun and a Royal Navy gunner allocated to each ship. The convoys were also protected by accompanying Royal Navy ships.

The Merchant Navy and their allies suffered huge losses by both U-boat and air attacks. The Registrar General of Shipping and Seamen calculated that of the 185,000 merchant seamen serving on British registered ships during the war, 27 per cent, almost 50,000 seamen, died through enemy action. This was the highest casualty rate of the armed forces. On the 31st August 1940, only a month after Drummond left to join the SS *Bonita*, the SS *Har Zion* was travelling in convoy to America when torpedoes fired from the U-boat, U-38, struck the ship. It sank with the loss of the master, 34 crewmen and one gunner. A single crewman survived.[23]

Attacks became commonplace, enemy submarines and planes stalked their every move. Drummond recalled that one morning, as she came on deck there was a "*terrific bang*". A ship moving anchorage struck a mine; as she watched, the ship's foremast crumpled and the vessel sank in two minutes. "*It was an awful sight, one minute here, the next minute gone.*"

In 1940 the SS *Bonita* was part of a convoy from Halifax, laden with scrap metal to assist the war effort at home. Such was the ferocity of the enemy on the crossing that only four vessels out of 39 survived the journey, limping into Port Talbot, South Wales on 5th November.[24]

In August 1940, Drummond, now second engineer, travelled in convoy to America with the SS *Bonita* when her ship "*... was attacked*

The SS Bonita Under-Fire.
© *David Alexander.*

for twenty-five minutes by German bombers, when four hundred miles from land".

On the 10th July 1941, *The Times* announced Drummond's award of an MBE for bravery. *John Bull* magazine reported: "*Miss Drummond looked around the gauges and machinery. The ship is running now, as fast as she can — faster than ever before, and so she ordered the engine room and stokehold staff out, and stayed there alone amid the damage, keeping her engines running full, taking all the risk herself. The men did not want to go. But Queen Victoria's godchild was not one to tolerate mutiny on the high seas! And out they had to go.*"[25]

The ships' mate wrote his account detailing her part in surviving the attack: "When the alarm gongs went, she went at once and took charge down below. After the first salvo which flung her against the levers and nearly stunned her, she realised that there was little hope. … in ten minutes, she had 'talked' to those engines to such good purpose that our miserable top speed of nine knots had risen to twelve and a half. That speed had never been recorded in all the ship's eighteen years".[26]

When they landed at Norfolk, Virginia, Drummond received a heroine's welcome. She accepted an invitation to speak to the townspeople on the hardships that British housewives were enduring. The local people collected money and a presentation was made to Drummond, who decided that it should go to her sisters and the people of Lambeth North.

Jean and Frances had remained in Lambeth during the Blitz, and played their parts as air raid wardens in the AFS. London was bombed almost every night for eight months. In that period, all of the houses the sisters lived or worked in were hit by bombs. The worst when a sub-fire station they were based in received a direct hit. Thirty-four people died. Thirty-three of whom were auxiliaries. Jean and Frances were buried in the rubble for five hours before being brought out, miraculously, with no serious injury.[27]

Situated just past Westminster Bridge, under the railway arches, the bright green liveried the *Victoria A. Drummond British–American Restaurant* became a beacon of hope to the blitzed people of Lambeth. The kitchens, equipped using the money from Norfolk, Virginia, fed 350 Londoners every day. One woman said "*… we needed a place like this. You can get a first-class meal for sixpence; meat and two vegetables. And isn't it funny when you come to think that she's a Lambeth girl too?*". After the war, Drummond hosted a visit by a group of ladies from Virginia who had subscribed to the restaurant.[28] [29]

The three sisters remained in Lambeth, now at 160 Kennington Road where they lived for the remainder of their lives.

In 1941, from Gibraltar, the *Bonita* joined a convoy headed across the Atlantic bound for the Clyde when a large four-engine bomber swooped on them from out of the clouds

Victoria wrote in her diary: "The first attack put the engine room telegraph out of action. I was off watch at the time and dashed down below to find the engine room full of steam and ash, I thought a boiler had gone, but it hadn't. … The plane came in again with machine gun attack. James Clegg, one of the quartermasters was machine gunned and died in the arms of a young Romanian boy. Skylight glasses, the mirror on the wheelhouse, the bridge clock and telescope, were all smashed up. … the engine room was a fearful mess. The bridge was open to the four winds with only a canvas wind-dodger in front of the wheel since all the wheelhouse was shot away".

Only by being able to coax as much speed as possible from the old engines did the captain outmanoeuvre the German bomber successfully.[30]

Even in her quieter times, Drummond continued to be a source of news for both the editorial pages and society columns. In July 1941, Drummond received her MBE from King George VI at an investiture in Buckingham Palace.[31] This was followed in October with the award of the Lloyd's War Medal for Exceptional Gallantry at Sea. Newspapers also reported that when on shore leave, Miss Drummond liked nothing better than spending time with her two sisters in their Lambeth flat and "… *wearing frilly clothes. They are such a luxury after an old greasy boiler suit in the engine-room*". Her hobby, it seems, was fishing for sharks, which she did with some success in Aden and Hobart. [32] Indeed, she had long experience with a rod and line – in 1914 she was recorded as landing a 24lb salmon on the opening week of the salmon season on the River Tay.[33]

In 1944 Victoria joined the MV *Karabagh* and took part in at least one Russian convoy. The Russian convoys were the most arduous and hazardous of journeys undertaken by merchant seamen. Ships had to maintain their position in their convoy or risk being 'picked off' by a waiting enemy. Working in extreme cold and heavy seas made this exhaustingly difficult, with the result that losses were high, in some crossings, as many as 60 percent of the ships were lost.

The MV *Karabagh* was given an important role in the invasion of Normandy. Operation Overlord, as it was known, began on the 6th June, where in excess of 7,000 vessels disembarked over one million allied troops onto the beaches. The MV *Karabagh* was stationed off the Isle of White and on 'special ops', as Drummond put it. She thought of them as smugglers, ferrying back and forth with fuel and supplies to help sustain the invasion, sailing at night to avoid enemy attention. "*It was a difficult and dangerous time as there were enemy planes everywhere.*" These special ops lasted until 9th September.

In May 1945, the *Karabagh* was lying off Antwerp when the Allies declared victory. Ships all around celebrated by setting off rockets and tracer bullets, but, loaded with 10,000 tonnes of high aviation spirit, the *Karabagh* had to signal to the others to stop in case they all blew up.

Drummond wrote, "I thought of my friends on the *Har Zion* and on the *Perseus*, and all our many friends lost in the Lambeth raids, and of other cousins and other wars. ... but I was alive, Jean and Frances had survived and we had won the war".

After Antwerp, they were the first ship into Kiel, travelling slowly up the Kiel Canal following minesweepers. The devastation shocked Drummond. "*It was flattened, bombed to bits. ... There was a lot of typhoid about and we were told not to go ashore, but of course I did. It was beginning to get dark as I came back through a wood and suddenly, I heard a sharp whistling sound as something cleared my head. It was a bullet from a sniper. ... after that I didn't go ashore again.*" From Kiel, the *Karabagh* escorted captured and prized German naval ships back to Scotland as commodore ship, which meant that the captain of

*Victoria Drummond on receiving the MBE for exceptional gallantry at sea.
Presented on 4th July 1941 by King George VI. From an original copy of The War
Illustrated, Volume Nine. Published by The Amalgamated Press, London, 1946.*

the *Karabagh* was in charge of the good order of the merchant ships in the convoy.

When the reality of her circumstances after the war took hold, Drummond had to take stock of her life. She seriously considered taking the Board of Trade First Engineer Certificate. If she had such a certificate, the ships she would work on would be of a much better condition and quality. However, afraid the Board would look for excuses to fail her again, she left things as they were, continuing to find work using her Panamanian certificate.

Through her past service with the Blue Funnel Line, Drummond found work supervising the construction of two 10,000-ton vessels at the Caledon Yard in Dundee. After that two-year period ashore, Drummond moved from ship to ship, often working on tramp-steamers; working boats without fixed schedules, carrying whatever cargo they could manage.

It was a hard life; for Drummond, now in her mid-60s, was forced to work on boats which, by their very nature, were at the lower end of the market. These vessels often came with a history of poor maintenance, resulting in a greater demand for her skills. Skills that were often not appreciated by younger engineers, who on occasion were openly physically aggressive to orders from a woman. However, she looked upon these confrontations as an unfortunate part of the job she loved that she had to cope with.

One of these ships was the *Eastern Med*, with an Egyptian crew, captained by 71-year-old ex-naval officer Willie Rogers. Rogers commented that Miss Drummond was, "*Quiet, efficient, and minds her job, … and I have to mind my language. … she is a fine gal*". Because Drummond didn't drink or smoke, for the ritual of sharing a tot of rum at the end of the day, Rogers made sure that they had a tin of cocoa on board for his chief.[34]

Very much a bonus of the job was travelling the world. She went ashore when she could, especially when she could indulge herself with a visit to a local hotel for a properly hot bath. She talked to the local people when she could, visited tourist attractions, or simply wandered the streets admiring the buildings.

It was a hard and, at times, dangerous world for a woman on her own. Over the years, she had several accidents at sea, breaking many ribs and bones and many other 'little' inconveniences that she shrugged off as part of her job. In Greece, three men attacked her, attempting to drag her off the road into waste ground. She fought them off biting, kicking, using her shoes as weapons and shouting at them till people nearby heard and came to assist.

None of this stopped her from looking for her next berth.

In February 1962, Drummond ended her 40 years at sea in Hong Kong. She had served on 39 ships, starting as a tenth engineer, ending her nautical days as first engineer. This was a career in which she made many round-the-world voyages, regularly visiting ports in all corners of the globe.

In her later life, as she reached 80 years old, she developed problems with her mobility and memory. Her sisters – Jean, four years older, and Frances, three years younger – devotedly looked after her until, in 1974, she fell out of bed and broke her leg. After some resistance, Drummond was admitted to St Thomas's Hospital. The sisters visited her twice a day in all weathers, but the resulting strain caused both of them to become ill. They were both admitted to the same hospital as their sister. Tragically, Jean and Frances passed away within two days of each other.

A confused Drummond, finding it difficult to accept that her beloved sisters were no longer with her, was transferred to St George's Retreat, Burgess Hill in East Sussex on 5th January 1975. Here, looked after by Augustinian nuns, Drummond spent the last years of her life before passing away on Christmas Day 1978 at the age of 84. Sister Thomas, now the Chair of the Trustees, wrote in March 2020, *"I was part of the team that cared for her, she was a very strong character* and was able to tell us of her very challenging career, but did not mention the MBE."

Victoria Drummond MBE, is buried at Megginch Castle alongside her parents and sisters.

In 1926, on her certification, Victoria Drummond became the first female member of the Institute of Marine Engineers (now known as IMarEST), in whose London headquarters now exists a Victoria Drummond Room. Her niece and biographer, Cherry Drummond, who took the title of Baroness Strange, wrote that the highlights of Victoria's life were attending the Institute of Marine Engineers' annual meetings. "*Even today there are people who remember the old lady who listened avidly and took notes in an old exercise book. They did not know who she was, and she did not know that one day, there would be a room in that self-same Institute named in her honour; the Victoria Drummond Room.*"

Drummond was awarded an MBE for bravery, presented by George VI in July 1941 at an investiture at Buckingham Palace. She was accompanied by her sisters, Jean and Frances.

In October 1941, Victoria became the first woman to receive a Lloyd's War Medal for Exceptional Gallantry at Sea.

In February 1943, an American publication, *True Comics Press*, issue #21, included a six-page cartoon story titled, *Victoria Drummond – The Lady is an Engineer.*[35]

Shortly after her death in 1978, the National Union of Marine, Aviation and Shipping Transport Officers, now known as Nautilus International, instituted the Victoria Drummond Award in memory of the "… *pioneering first female marine engineer.*", to be awarded no more than once every four years to a lady member who has distinguished herself in the field of marine or aviation service.[36]

On 14th October 1994, a book celebrating her life, *The Remarkable Life of Victoria Drummond Marine Engineer*, written by her niece Cherry Drummond, also known as Baroness Strange, was launched on the centenary of her birth at Megginch Castle.[37]

In 2013 Victoria featured in the *Women of Science, celebrating trailblazers of the past* exhibition at the National Library of Scotland.[38]

Also in 2013, a plaque in her name was fixed at the entrance to Abertay University, Dundee, which is part of the Dundee Global Trail.[39]

In 2018 Victoria Drummond was inducted into the Scottish Engineering Hall of Fame.[40]

"Women make good sailors. As many women are born with the love of the sea as men. Women endure hardships admirably, better than men as a rule. They are wonderful when put to the test of courage. I'd like to live the greater part of my life on the sea. It is the healthiest life in the world. I enjoy being a ship engineer in overalls far more than being a society do-nothing."[41]

The family burial ground at Megginch Castle. Victoria Alexandrina Drummond's final resting place. With permission of Catherine Drummond-Herdman.
© Catherine Drummond-Herdman.

References

1   *Northern Whig*, 24th December 1921, p. 4. Col. 7.
2   *The Courier*, 9th March 1923, p. 8. col. 1.
3   *The Evening News*, 1st May 1936, p. 8. col. 8.
4   Drummond, Cherry, *The Remarkable Life of Victoria Drummond Marine Engineer* (London, 1999). p. 36.
5   Drummond, *The Remarkable Life of Victoria Drummond*, p. 56.
6   Drummond, *The Remarkable Life of Victoria Drummond*, p. 56.
7   Devils Porridge Museum, https://www.devilsporridge.org.uk/miss-j-drummond-a-life-of-striking-contrasts
8   British Red Cross. https://www.redcross.org.uk
9   *Dundee Courier*, 18th March 1994, p. 7. col. 1.
10 *Sheffield Daily Telegraph*, 12th December 1921, p. 8. col. 6.
11 *The Sunday Post*, 23rd July 1922, p. 11. col. 5.
12 Australasian Institute of Marine and Power Engineers, *Forty-Second Report. For year ending June 1923.*
13 *Montrose Standard*, 19th January 1923, p. 6. col. 6.
14 *Penrith Observer*, 6th March 1923, p. 6. col. 7.
15 *Yorkshire Evening Post*, 7th February 1923, p. 6. col. 4.
16 *The Courier*, 30th May 1924, p. 8. col. 4.
17 *John Bull*, 16th October 1926, p.12. col. 3.
18 https://www.undiscoveredscotland.co.uk/usbiography/d/victoriadrummond.html
19 Drummond, Cherry, *The Remarkable Life of Victoria Drummond Marine Engineer*, (London, 1999). p. 165–170.
20 Conversation with Catherine Drummond-Herdman. 4th August 2021.
21 *The Scotsman*, 22nd June 1938, p. 11. col. 3.
22 *Dundee Courier*, 29th July 1940, p. 3. col. 1.
23 Details of merchant ships lost to U-boats. https://www.uboat.net
24 Ships in Atlantic convoys. https://www.warsailors.com/convoys
25 *The People*, 28th September 1941, p. 3. col. 6.
26 *John Bull*, 16th August 1941, p. 7.
27 https://www.devilsporridge.org.uk/miss-j-drummond-a-life-of-striking-contrasts
28 *The People*, 28th September 1941, p. 3. col. 6.
29 *Belfast Newsletter*, 15th July 1941, Page 3.
30 *The Courier and Advertiser*, 10th July 1941, p. 2. col. 5.
31 *The War Illustrated*. 4th July 1941, Vol 4, No. 96. p. 650.
32 *Blyth News Ashington Post*, 10th July 1941, p. 2 col. 8.
33 *The Aberdeen Press and Journal*. 21st April 1914, p. 10. col. 2.
34 *Daily Mirror*, 3rd May 1948, p. 5. Col. 6.
35 *The Lady is an Engineer*. (True Comics Press. Issue #21, pp. 57–62. 1943)
36 *Victoria Drummond Award*, presented to women whose achievements raise the profile of women at sea. https://www.nautilusint.org/en/our-union/what-we-do/recognising-achievement/
37 *Perthshire Advertiser*, 30th September 1994, p. 21. Col. 2.
38 *National Library of Scotland*. https://www.nls.uk/learning-zone/science-and-technology/women-scientists/victoria-drummond/
39 *Mapping Memorials to Women of Scotland*. https://www.womenofscotland.org.uk
40 *Scottish Engineering Hall of Fame*. https://www.engineeringhalloffame.org/profile/victoria-alexandrina-drummond
41 *Derry Journal*, 8th May 1935, p. 8. col. 3.

James Finlayson,
© David Alexander.

James Finlayson

JAMES Henderson Finlayson was born in Larbert, Stirlingshire on 27th August 1877. His father, Alexander, was a local man and a blacksmith, while his mother, Isabella Wood Henderson, came from Stonehaven, in the parish of Dunnottar, Kincardineshire. The family home was known as Dunnottar Cottage, 9 Victoria Road, Larbert.

The young Finlayson first worked as an apprentice tinsmith at the Torwood Foundry alongside his father. In the draft registration form he filed shortly after arriving in the United States, Finlayson stated he had lost two toes on his right foot. Perhaps an accident at work persuaded him that a life in industry wasn't for him.

As a leading member of the Larbert Dramatic Club, he had an interest in theatre before he met theatre producer John Clyde, but as a member of Clyde's theatre company, he was introduced into the wider world of theatre and acting and played a variety of roles in local repertory, music hall, and as a character actor with the Theatre Royal, Edinburgh.[1]

However, it was in music hall that he shone, with many of his scenes written by Alec Lauder, brother of Harry Lauder. Later, in America, Finlayson worked not only with Alec again, but with two of John Clyde's sons, David and Andrew, who both settled in California and had fine acting careers.

By 1896, Alexander and Isabella had nine children; life would have been a desperate struggle. By the end of 1909, tragedy had hit the family with the deaths of both parents: Isabella in 1903, aged 42, and Alexander in 1909 at the age of 57. By the time of their father's death, the family had also lost three of their siblings: Agnes Wilson in 1884, aged three; Annie Gay in 1887, aged one; and only a month before her father, Isabella Wood died just a few days short of her 28th birthday.

The death of their parents, and sisters, must have been a tremendous blow to Finlayson and the surviving siblings. With work almost impossible to find in a Scotland gripped by a severe economic depression, Finlayson and his siblings felt they had no alternative but to emigrate. They made plans to move the entire family to a new life in America.

An older cousin, David Finlayson, had already made this move, settling in Garry, Indiana, but returned to Larbert in the midst of the family turmoil in 1909. He made the journey back to the USA the following year and took a flat in 1401 Bedford Ave, Brooklyn, New York. In October of the same year, 20-year-old Jeanie made the crossing, joining a cousin in New Jersey.

By 1930 approximately 10 per cent of the Scottish workforce had emigrated to Australia, New Zealand or North America. Scots were not alone; mass migration to the United States began around 1880, reaching a peak in 1907 when approximately 1.25 million immigrants were processed at Ellis Island.

Finlayson landed on Ellis Island on 27th May 1911 with his 17-year-old brother Robert, moving to join Uncle David in New York. While Robert declared himself an engineer, Finlayson, forsaking his training as a tinsmith, now looked upon himself as a professional actor.

Five months later, David's wife Effie brought their daughter, with the two youngest Finlayson girls, Agnes Ann, age 19, and 15-year-old Effie, to join her husband in an apartment at 619 49th Street, Brooklyn. Finlayson and Robert were also living there at this time.

It wasn't until 1926 that elder brother Alexander arrived to join the family. Around 1912, he had made the trip from Scotland to Canada, marrying before making the border crossing into the United States with his 13-year-old son, also Alexander. Landing at Port Huron in

Michigan, their manifest papers stated they were going to stay with brother James Finlayson, c/o Hal Roach Studios. All six surviving siblings were now together.

Later in his life, when Finlayson returned to visit and work in the United Kingdom, he was able to make the journey as a first-class passenger. On his first trip across the Atlantic with his brother, they travelled as, what was then termed, second-cabin passengers. The conditions were cramped, and even though they had basic facilities and food, second-cabin passengers were restricted to their own area below deck for the duration of the 10-day trip. Given the level of seasickness caused by the continual buffeting of heavy Atlantic seas while confined to the depths of the ship, this would have made for a very uncomfortable journey indeed.

Robert and Alexander found work in the growing film industry as camera technicians. Agnes, recorded in the census of 1920 as staying at Finlayson's home at 283 West Fifth Street, worked as a stenographer at a local YMCA.

Fortunately, the experience Finlayson gained working in Scottish repertory theatre and music hall stood him in good stead. He quickly landed the role as the title character's father in Graham Moffat's Scottish comedy, *Bunty Pulls the Strings,* which opened at Colliers Comedy Theatre on Broadway on 10th October 1912. It was a huge success, running for 18 months and 391 performances.

After Broadway, Finlayson joined a vaudeville company about to embark on a nationwide tour of America, coincidentally reuniting with Alec Lauder who had also made the move from Scotland. They toured constantly until, after four years on the road, the company came to play in California.

In 1919 Finlayson married Emily Cora Gilbert from Iowa, who also lived in Los Angeles. He was almost 32 years old while Emily was 19. Married for only a few years, Cora and Finlayson divorced at some point before July 1925, when records show Emily remarried.

Hollywood was a city in the early days of the film industry and Finlayson, determined to work in this growing new media, left the tour. Minor parts came first at the L-KO Studio and then with the Thomas Ince Studio until, in 1920, four years after arriving in Hollywood, he landed a three-year contract with the Mack Sennett Comedies Corporation. Sennett was the creator of the enormously popular Keystone Kops and the originator of slapstick routines.

With Sennett, Finlayson worked with some of the biggest names in Hollywood; when he made a naturalisation application in 1924, his referees were Ben Turpin and Charlie Chase. This application was declined. Another eighteen years passed before he was accepted as an American citizen.

In this period, Finlayson appeared in several films with comic legend Ben Turpin, playing opposite as the villain or straight man to Turpin's trademark cross-eyed comic character. However, it wasn't until 1923, when he joined film producer Hal Roach at his Culver City Studios, that he was given the opportunity to have top billing.

Alongside Finlayson, two other young aspiring comic actors, Oliver Hardy and Stan Laurel were on contract with Roach, each pursuing solo careers, but Roach could see potential in all three, and set about creating the best combination for the screen.

Initially, Finlayson played the antagonist in nineteen of Stan Laurel's early solo films with a further five alongside Oliver Hardy, which led Roach to promote him to lead in three short films in 1925 and 1926, with Stan Laurel directing. However, these films were not as successful as Roach had hoped, and for a short period, it was thought Laurel, Hardy and Finlayson would film as a trio with equal billing. Indeed, one short of 1927, *Love 'em and Weep*, gives cast credit as Stan Laurel, James Finlayson and Oliver Hardy.

Roach, however, decided the starring combination would be Laurel and Hardy; a pairing that film fans the world over took to their hearts, and who worked together for the rest of their careers. By this time, Finlayson had perfected his trademark mannerisms: a long double-take which faded away, a squint, and a one-eyed stare with raised eyebrows, all perfect for the anarchic style of silent film. James Finlayson appeared in 35 Laurel and Hardy films. Films often billed as 'Laurel and Hardy with James Finlayson'. [2]

Billed as James but known to his friends as Jimmie, Finlayson was known around the studio as Jim or Fin. Ross Owen, movie historian and consultant to the 2019 film, *Stan and Ollie*, notes Stan Laurel always called him Jimmie, "*... in fact, Stan's daughter Lois, always referred to James as Uncle Jimmie*".

Finlayson had established himself as an important cast member in the majority of the Laurel and Hardy feature films, including a standout performance as Mickey Finn in *Way Out West* in 1937.

Simon Louvish, author of *Stan and Ollie, The Roots of Comedy* and *The Double Life of Laurel and Hardy*, wrote of Finlayson: "*Who can forget Fin, the balding, moustached and often seething Scot, master*

James Finlayson with Stan Laurel and Oliver Hardy in Another Fine Mess. Film Fun Annual. Published by Amalgamated Press Ltd. London, 1939.

of the double and triple take, whom many would regard as the third member of the Laurel and Hardy team – the indispensable foil ..."[3]

Finlayson's drawn-out exclamation, preceded by an exasperated look to camera, of "*d'ohhhhh*", inspired Dan Castellaneta, the voice actor who plays Homer Simpson, to give Homer his trademark exclamation of "*d'oh*". Castellaneta explained that while the long drawn out "*d'ohhhhh*" of Jimmie Finlayson was perfect for film of his era, animation required a quicker response and created the shortened version, "*d'oh*". The word has since been accepted by the Oxford Dictionary and is commonly used by someone who realises they have just said or done something stupid.[4]

Where many others had failed, Finlayson made the transition from silent to sound, and from black and white to colour, continuing to find work when tastes and styles changed. No longer did movies have to feature madcap action and over-the-top exaggerated acting to attract an audience. With sound, there could be more considered dialogue and less frenetic action, forcing Finlayson to adapt as the technology evolved.

In a feature on the Laurel and Hardy website in 2009 titled, *Ask Lois Laurel-Hawes*, Stan Laurel's daughter tells of Finlayson's friendship with her father, "*Jimmie and his girlfriend Stephanie came to the house often. But never wearing his moustache! I don't think a lot of people recognised him with the moustache off*". Although he was best known for his trademark moustache, it was false, and he appeared many times on screen without it. In another letter she answers, "*Of course Jimmie Finlayson, like Babe Hardy, was as close as any family member could be*".[5]

Finlayson kept in touch with his Scottish roots, having regular copies of the local *Falkirk Herald* posted to him in Hollywood, and he returned to Scotland when work permitted. *The Herald* reported in August 1935, "*The Hollywood laughter-maker has acquired a big bagful of braw golf clubs. He plays quite a decent game. During his four days' visit he played two rounds over the Tryst course. Jimmy is to be in London for six weeks yet. Since his arrival here he has made two pictures, and has another to make before he goes home".*[6]

In 1935, a review of Finlayson's film, *What Happened to Harkness?* reminds readers that *"… it marked his return to the screen as a 'Keystone Cop,' a role he made famous in the old Keystone comedy days. It was also his 250th film, which must be practically a record for any artist."*[7]

Returning to Hollywood from Britain in September 1939, Finlayson was astounded to be met on the platform at Pasadena Station by Laurel and Hardy dressed in kilts, accompanied by a line of Scottish pipers. Finlayson, flanked by Stan and Ollie, then triumphantly led the way from the station through the adoring crowds.[8]

Finlayson continued to be offered character parts in feature films until illness forced his retirement from a busy work schedule in 1951, although he continued to work for the rest of his life.[9]

Stephen Rettie, the Finlayson family biographer, reports that in September 1939 the engagement was announced between Finlayson and English actress Stephanie Insall. They never married, but for 20 years he had breakfasted with Stephanie at her home in Franklin Avenue, until one particular morning Finlayson didn't turn up. Out of character for Finlayson, she went to his home to investigate, only to find that he had died during the night.

James Henderson Finlayson died of a heart attack in his sleep at his home, 1966 Beachwood Drive, Los Angeles, California on 9th October 1953, age 66.

An active Freemason and Past Master of the Lodge, Finlayson was cremated on the same afternoon at the Masonic Chapel in Hollywood with Masonic honours. Producer Mack Sennett; fellow Keystone Cop, Hank Mann; Billy Bevan; Snub Pollard; Tom Kennedy; and Andy Clyde, son of John Clyde who introduced Finlayson to acting, were amongst fellow actors and filmmakers present.[10]

Stan Laurel and Oliver Hardy were unable to attend, as they were

James Finlayson with Stan Laurel and Oliver Hardy in Another Fine Mess.
Film Fun Annual.
Published by Amalgamated Press Ltd. London, 1939.

at the beginning of a series of shows around Britain. Hardy suffered a heart attack in May 1954, bringing the tour to a halt. The Palace Theatre in Plymouth became the last stage where Laurel and Hardy performed.

James Finlayson arrived in Hollywood at the birth of a new medium of film which took the world by storm. He was a central character in many of the early movies, starring alongside a host of the biggest stars of the era, many of whom became close friends. *The Stage*, a British newspaper covering the entertainment industry, called him "*The unsung hero of Laurel and Hardy films*".

An 'oasis' of the *Sons of the Desert*, an international Laurel and Hardy appreciation society, named after the 1933 film bearing the same name, was formed in Glasgow in 2019 by, and for, relations of Finlayson named, *Our relations tent of James Finlayson*.

A plaque by the Scottish Film Council honouring James Finlayson was displayed by Bo'ness Library as part of their Hippfest 2019 Silent Film Festival.

In the Scottish Football Cup Final between Falkirk and Inverness Caledonian Thistle in June 2015, a group of Falkirk fans, based in Winsford, Cheshire, calling themselves The Sons of Finlay unveiled a large banner bearing the image of Finlayson to bolster support for his local team. It didn't work; Falkirk lost by two goals to one. James Finlayson would have muttered, "*d'oh!*" [11]

References

1   *Falkirk Herald*,17th October 1953, p. 6. col. 6.
2   Laurel & Hardy Society. https://www.wayoutwest.org
3   Louvish, Simon, *Stan and Ollie The Roots of Comedy* (London, 2001). p. 156.
4   *The Sunday Herald*, 21st Jul 2007.
5   *Ask Lois Laurel-Hayes*. www.laurel-and-hardy.com/dyk/asklois.html
6   *Falkirk Herald*, 19th August 1933, p.6. col. 6.
7   *Bexon and Oxon Advertiser*, 16th August 1935, p. 8. col. 3.
8   *Aberdeen People's Journal*, 30th September 1939, p. 6. col. 2.
9   *The Stage*, 7th August 1997, P. 8. col. 1.
10 *Falkirk Herald*, 24th October 1953, p. 6. col. 6.
11 Sons of Finlay tribute to their hero. https://youtu.be/uwC8XPekMVE

Beatrice Clugston. c1882. From a portrait by Robert Crawford. (1842–1924)
With permission of Auld Kirk Museum and East Dunbartonshire Leisure and
Culture Trust. © East Dunbartonshire Leisure and Culture Trust.

Beatrice Clugston

BEATRICE Clugston was born on 19th September 1827 in Glasgow's Barony Parish, most likely at 22 Monteith Row, Calton. She was the first child of John Clugston and Mary McKenzie who were married in Glasgow on 12th October 1826. They had five children, Beatrice, John, Agnes, William and Mary. Sadly, Agnes at three years of age; John aged four; and William, age unknown, died in early childhood.[1]

Like his father before him, John Clugston was a trained accountant and together they were involved in the Glasgow Galloway Brotherly Society from its foundation in 1791. The aim of the society was to financially support the families left behind in Galloway by the many from the region who made the move to Glasgow in search of work. The Clugstons were a large family with roots in Galloway.

Throughout her life, Mary Clugston was recognised as having been born in Jamaica. The Clugston family archive details that she was a daughter of Duncan MacKenzie Esq, *"... late of the parish of Westmorland in the County of Cornwall, Island of Jamaica."* In his will of 24th November 1842, he left his reputed daughters Mary, Elizabeth and Ann, £50 each for mourning. He ordered his estates at Camp Savana and Mountain Spring to be sold with the proceeds to be given to his wife Jessie McKenzie, and *"after her decease £500 to each of his children."*[2]

A reputed child was an illegitimate offspring who was recognised by the father. This implied that Mary Clugston's mother, was most likely enslaved. Mary Clugston's death certificate names her father as Duncan McKenzie, sugar planter, and Beatrice McKenzie, nee Morton as her mother. Beatrice appears to be named after her grandmother.[3] [4]

All the family involved themselves in philanthropic and religious societies in the Calton and Bridgeton areas of Glasgow, regularly attending the Bridgeton Presbyterian Church. John was the secretary of the Calton Society for Religious Purposes, which provided education to the poor, and distributed scriptures. He was also involved in the administration of both the Calton and Bridgeton Provident Banks.

John senior, followed by his son, were treasurers of the Calton Bread Society in the period 1810–1835. The Bread Society worked to try to break the high prices fixed by the bakery manufacturers' cartel; to aid the poorly paid and starving weavers. Protests by the Calton Weavers came to a head in the Calton Weavers Food Riots of 1816, which resulted in the army being deployed to forcibly subdue the rioters.

John Clugston, given his involvement with the people of Calton, would have had a role to play in the aftermath of the riots.

A notice in the *Edinburgh Gazette* on 20th March 1849, and a further notice on the 30th April, declared that, "the copartnery business carried out in Glasgow as Manufacturer and Merchants and at Avon Bank as Bleachers under the firm of John King and Sons was this day dissolved by mutual consent of the subscribers, sole partners, therein. The subscriber, John Clugston is authorised to uplift and discharge all debts to the company.

It seems that John Clugston had, at some time, taken a half-share of the business and now took ownership of the business, resulting in the family relocating to Larkhall. The 1851 census details the family living at Avonbank, in the village of Millheugh, Larkhall, describing John Clugston as a power loom bleacher and manufacturer, employing 21 men, 18 women and 2 boys. He not only manufactured cotton but completed the bleaching process, or whitening of the cloth, in his own factory.

John Clugston died suddenly on 27th March 1855, of "*chronic disease of the brain*", which, as noted on his death certificate, had been diagnosed two years previously.[5]

John had two brothers, William and James. They were also office bearers of the Glasgow Galloway Brotherly Society and it is thought likely they were involved with in the textile industry in Calton and John's project in Larkhall.

A short time after her husband's death in 1855, Mary moved the family back to Landsdowne Crescent in Glasgow's West End. Beatrice was around 28 years old at this time. Beatrice's sister Mary, now being recognised as Mary Morton Clugston, her only surviving sibling, passed away at this address on 3rd November 1859 at the age of 24, leaving Beatrice and her mother as the remaining members of the family.

Beatrice is described by local historians as a young lady, short and dumpy, who talked a lot and who could be bossy and very religious. However, she was certainly the worthiest person in any room and could convince any man to contribute a considerable sum to one of her causes.[6]

For all of her life, both her parents engaged with charitable and religious institutions; much more so for her father in the last two years of his life. Perhaps John Clugston dealt with the knowledge of an incurable brain disease by throwing himself with extra vigour into work for the church, a vigour that Clugston continued after her father's death.

Clugston, with no specific training or profession, committed her life to charitable causes, joining her mother's visits to the North Prison and the Magdalene Institution in Glasgow around 1860. Shortly after this, she became a visitor to impoverished patients at the Glasgow Royal Infirmary. Her experiences in both institutions, were to change her life.

In 1864 she formed a Dorcas Society. Based in the Glasgow Royal Infirmary, the Society took their name from the Old Testament story of Dorcas, who made clothes for the widow of Joppa and carried out good works for the poor. The first Dorcas Society in Britain was founded in 1834 on the Isle of Man. Generally, these societies were not connected to one another, having usually been organised informally by women, often the wives of doctors, as a social group.[7]

Normally, when the poorest in society were admitted to hospital, the clothes they stood in – for many, their only belongings – were burned to prevent infection. It was for these people that the Dorcas Society and Almoners Fund, to give it its full name, was formed to provide the necessities needed to aid their recovery.

In 1860 there were neither facilities, nor any kind of convalescence for patients being discharged. Clugston, appalled at the hardship this caused, began plans for purpose-built premises to which patients could be transferred from hospital. A place in which to recover in preparation for a return to their own home. This was a far different proposition from persuading a few like-minded people to give up a little of their time to provide food and clothes. To make such a difference, a significant sum of money would be needed. Deciding to raise her funds through bazaars, Clugston discovered she had a talent for fundraising.

Bazaars were advertised in advance, announcing the contents of the tables along with the titles of the ladies who took charge of each table. The higher the rank or status in society, the more attractive the tables became, and when HRH Princess Louise showed an interest in Clugston's cause, both the public and society were thrilled. [8]

Princess Louise was the sixth of Queen Victoria's nine children, and certainly the most rebellious and controversial. She had a great interest in the arts and education, supported women's suffrage, and became a very talented artist and sculptor. Rejecting arranged marriages with foreign princes, she married a Scot, John Campbell, Marquis of Lorne, becoming the first royal since Tudor times to marry outside of royalty. As heir to the Argyle title, after his father died in 1900, the couple took the titles of the Duke and Duchess of Argyle.

When Princess Louise attended Clugston's bazaar in November

1871, the royal couple travelled from Erskine House in Renfrewshire, in an open carriage drawn by four grey horses, to the City Halls in the centre of Glasgow. During the First World War, the house became the Princess Louise Hospital for Limbless Sailors and Soldiers, and is now the five-star Marr Hall Hotel. Such was the princess's popularity that cheering crowds lined the route.

The princess, a patron of many charities and causes, was genuinely interested in Clugston's work, and with her patronage she brought a bank draft from Queen Victoria for 100 guineas as a contribution to the fund. With royal approval from the Queen herself, and the personal patronage of the princess, those at the very highest levels of society became ever more eager to contribute to Clugston's work. When advertising the bazaar held in St Andrew's Halls, the organisers apologised that, *"Owing to the very large number of ladies who have consented to take part in the bazaar, the promoters ... have found it impractical to fulfil their original intention of publishing the whole of the names of the Ladies of Rank who have kindly agreed to be Patronesses."* The advert could find space to name only duchesses, countesses and marchionesses. The prospect of being attended by, or even mingling with, members of the upper class, along with the possibility of being in the same room as a member of the royal family, ensured huge numbers of the public attended.[9]

An important part of Clugston's life was to share the joy of her Christian principles. To the ladies who attended the many bible reading meetings she gave, Clugston was an inspiration, instilling in them a belief that as Christian women it was their duty to help the poor and afflicted of society. This network of bible ladies, ladies of rank, and ladies of title, laid the foundation of her successful fundraising enterprises.

In her bazaars, tables were themed, with the ladies at each table taking the responsibility for sourcing and acquiring the items they would sell. This resulted in a wide variety of goods from the most basic of household items to the more exotic, such as drawing room ornaments, items for personal embellishment, sofas, fire screens, smoking caps, dolls, toys, boxes, pictures, vases, flowers, Christmas trees and even wax babies. Food and drink were also available in abundance and, by the time her later bazaars came along, an enormous number of additional items were available, such as books, clothing, feathers, oils for hair, pomades, soaps, toilet sets in china, and ivory ornaments. Food available ranged from butter and biscuits, cheese, deer, game, herring in barrels, lobsters, oysters, rabbit, and all sorts of teas, fruits and preserves.

Through the Dorcas Society at the Glasgow Royal Infirmary, along with assistance from the Lord Provost of Glasgow, a bazaar was planned to raise funds for the Glasgow Convalescent Home at Bothwell. Glasgow Council not only provided the use of the City Halls without charge, but set aside a generous amount to decorate the interior. Their actions set a standard. The décor was praised to such a high degree that subsequent bazaars were designed to satisfy the high expectations of the public.[10]

The bazaar was an outstanding success. Opening on the 14th December 1864, it ran for four days, attracting between four and five thousand people each day; such was the crush at times that the doors had to be closed until it became safe to allow entry to more of the public. The total sum received was £6,090.

In 1865, with additional subscriptions from wealthy patrons, the Glasgow Convalescent Home at Bothwell opened. The committee managed to acquire two adjoining villas on a five-year lease. With shared grounds, using one house for males and the other for females, the home could accommodate 30 patients on opening, with the expectation that 400 patients could be received annually. Each patron who subscribed to the sum of £10, or paid an annual subscription of one guinea, could nominate one person for treatment in the home.[11]

With her successful entry into the world of fundraising, Clugston thrived on new challenges. As she had no training to work in the hospitals, Clugston involved herself in the planning of each project before handing over the funds raised to directors who would then take over the day-to-day staffing and running of each facility. She also assisted in raising money for several existing charitable organisations: the Lochburn Home of the Glasgow Magdalene Institution (£700), the Samaritan Society based in the Western Infirmary, and the Sick Children's Hospitals in the city (£3,000), all benefited from her fundraising expertise.

Clugston's next project, again working with the Glasgow Royal Infirmary Dorcas Society, was to raise funds in aid of a Convalescent Fever Hospital and a Sick Children's Hospital. Opening on the 19th December 1866, the City Halls were set up in the style of an eastern bazaar, decorated to a Byzantine theme. The ladies managing the tables delighted the public with "… *oriental costumes to complete the illusion*". The sum raised by the final day was in the region of £5,400. [12] [13]

On 4th February 1869, Clugston proposed to local councillors the opening of a convalescent home on the Clyde Coast at Dunoon, that was later named the West of Scotland Convalescent Home. This was her biggest project to date, with very detailed fundraising aims: to remove the bond of £5,000 to allow the homes to be rent free, to raise £1,200 to furnish the homes, to introduce a system of saltwater baths, and to add 30 beds to the present accommodation. Clugston's wish was to be able to give each patient a course of treatment which lasted for three weeks.

A fundraising bazaar took place in Sauchiehall Street, Glasgow on 10th October 1870. Despite the scale of the project, Clugston managed to raise the £8,027 required, which allowed the home to open on 14th August 1869, barely five months after the initial announcement. One year after the opening, Princess Louise and her husband paid a visit to the home, travelling in their yacht from Roseneath and arriving at Dunoon pier, before travelling through immense crowds who lined the route to the home.

In later years, when Clugston paid visits to Dunoon, excited patients lined the pier to greet her arrival, with the atmosphere at the home akin to a gala day.

Her achievements attracted attention, not only from Scotland, but from all over the British Isles. On 20th September 1871, Florence Nightingale wrote, "*I write as soon as it is possible, and beg to enclose £10. 10s. I wish that the tiny sum (would that it were more, but if it were a hundred times as much, it would be still too small) could represent to you how great is the interest I feel in the success of your most useful of all useful undertakings – the Convalescent Home for the Poor. God speed them and you! Pray believe me, ever your faithful servant and theirs, Florence Nightingale.*"[14]

Florence Nightingale was a very popular and important figure at this time. Her groundbreaking work in caring for wounded soldiers in the Crimean War made her a national hero. Scotland offered no training for nurses; anyone looked upon as a nurse was someone who had gained their knowledge by experience, usually in their own community. In England, a similar situation had developed, leading to the opening of her first Nightingale Training School at St Thomas's Hospital in London in 1860. Nightingale nurses were highly respected, moving to other hospitals, passing on their knowledge, usually becoming the matron and immediately improving the dreadful conditions that existed in Victorian hospitals. It wasn't until 23rd December 1919 that the General Nursing Council (GNC) of Scotland joined the GNCs of England, Wales, and Ireland in establishing a register of nurses. At Glasgow Royal Infirmary, in a ground floor vestibule, stands a marble statue of Rebecca Strong, a Nightingale nurse and the first trained matron of the hospital in 1879.

After seven years, the directors of the Glasgow Convalescent

West of Scotland Convalescent Home, Dunoon.
From a Valentines Reliable Series postcard. 1905.
© Jerry Brannigan.

Home explained that the opening at Bothwell was always looked upon as an experiment and, as the project had been very successful, they decided the time had come to transfer the patients to new premises at Lenzie, to the north of Glasgow. Although the distance from Glasgow was much the same, the new railway station at Lenzie was within walking distance of the proposed new building. But perhaps more importantly for the directors, thanks to Clugston, they would own the building.[15]

She was now set with her biggest challenge to date. On 25th November 1871, she opened her latest bazaar in the Glasgow City Halls to raise money for the new convalescent home at Lenzie. This bazaar ran for four days and, given the public support of the much respected Florence Nightingale, along with the Patronage of the Duke and Duchess of Roxburghe, and the Duke and Duchess of Argyle, a high attendance was anticipated. The public didn't disappoint, raising the £6,500 required.

Earlier, around late 1870, land at Lenzie had been acquired, with James Thomson, one of the city's finest architects, commissioned to design a plain but substantial building, capable of holding 62 patients. The foundation stone was laid on 28th August 1871 by the Earl of Shaftesbury and, less than two years later, in 1873, the Glasgow Convalescent Home for the Glasgow Royal Infirmary opened. Expansion continued, and by 1900 the accommodation for patients had risen to 80 beds.

Clugston's next target was to establish a residential care home for those with incurable diseases. Broomhill House in Kirkintilloch, less than two miles from Lenzie, was available. Owner John Bartholomew, of the Edinburgh map publishing family, had died suddenly and his brother decided to sell the property. It was an ideal situation for Clugston; it was in good condition, already with extensions to both wings and set in an estate of 80 acres. However, before she could buy the estate, Clugston needed to raise yet more money.

This time they set the bazaar under the glass dome of Glasgow's magnificent Kibble Palace at the city's Botanic Gardens. Originally constructed at the home of Victorian entrepreneur and eccentric John Kibble, at Coulport on the shores of Loch Long, Kibble sold his 'Palace' to the Royal Botanic Institution of Glasgow in 1871. The many pieces were dismantled and moved to Glasgow by barge, where construction was completed in 1873.

The Kibble Palace was a huge success with the public. It is said that 6,000 people attended events staged inside the enormous glass dome, lit by 600 gas lamps, coloured for effect. Faced with the very best of merchandise – imported tableware and furniture, exotic food and fashionable art work – Clugston's bazaar again attracted a large and enthusiastic crowd. Scott Crawford, author of the book *The History of Broomhill and Lanfine Homes*, confirms that the precise

Broomhill Home for Incurables.
From The Graphic. 23rd October 1875.
© Jerry Brannigan.

BROOMHILL HOME FOR INCURABLES, NEAR GLASGOW

sum raised was £14,175 12s 2d. With the addition of further donations after the event, a total of £23,362 6s 7d was raised, ensuring that the purchase of the estate could go ahead.[16] [17]

In the early months of 1874, Clugston travelled to England, visiting many homes for convalescents and incurables, with the intent to find the best treatments to take back to her own homes. She wrote "*... but I did find in England what I have never seen in Scotland – homes, quiet resting-places provided for the dying: and I hope to see the day when, instead of the dying being dismissed from our hospitals, and hurried to their poor homes ... they will be taken to this and the other sweet home provided for them with loving hearts ... to give the dying a sweet impression of earth as they pass to heaven*".

Lord Shaftesbury inaugurated the Broomhill Estate purchase in 1875, and on 30th August 1876, the Lord Provost of Glasgow, Sir James Bain, formally opened Broomhill House, known as the Scottish National Institution for the Relief of Incurables.

They soon realised, as Florence Nightingale had suggested to Clugston, that many of these 'incurables' were just the opposite; with proper care and surroundings, the majority of their patients made full recoveries and were able to return to their homes and families.

By early 1876, having given all her time and energy to her causes, Clugston found herself with little money. Throughout all her campaigns and bazaars, with the exception of the campaign for the Broomhill Home for Incurables, where two ladies privately paid for her outlays, Clugston refused to deduct anything from the sums collected for her own expenses. Her mother said, "*Beatrice was constantly bringing in the halt, the lame, and the blind to be fed and clothed, with the consequence that her cupboards were bare and her carpets lasted no time*". The illnesses that had beset her in childhood returned, but undaunted, she continued to work for her causes. Supporters, who realised her situation, raised the sum of £3,116, which was, "... *spontaneously and privately raised by a few of her friends in the West of Scotland*".[18]

On the 28th November 1876, a celebration in the Religious Institution Rooms, Buchanan Street, Glasgow, gave thanks for the work Clugston had carried out, and a presentation of the funds raised was made. In accordance with her wishes, £2,500 was invested in Railway Stock with the balance of £916 paid by deposit receipt. This allowed Clugston and her mother to move from Glasgow city centre to Norwood, Moncrief Avenue, Lenzie. In addition, in the years before she died, her ladies arranged for a sum of money, which would provide her with an annuity to allow her to live in some comfort for the remainder of her life.[19]

In 1880, newspapers carried a notice that Clugston was going to speak on the "*Missing links in Scottish charities and how they may be put together*".[20] She announced a series of meetings throughout the city with guest speakers, ministers from local churches, who would celebrate the good works that all her ladies were carrying out.[21] Speaking of her plans for the future, she announced that a bazaar would be held in the St Andrews Halls, Glasgow in March 1881, with several objectives. She advocated building an extension Broomhill Home and the construction of Cottage Homes for those suffering from consumption, cancer and other incurable diseases who would not otherwise qualify for admission. This bazaar would also attempt to raise £6,000 to free a debt from the Dunoon Convalescent Home. The amount raised at this bazaar, as Scott Crawford again confirmed, was a grand total of £15,600. After the deduction of expenses, each institution received approximately £6,000.[22] [23]

In appreciation of her many charitable works, Clugston was presented with her portrait at the Glasgow Institute of Fine Arts in Sauchiehall Street, Glasgow on 12th December 1882. At a "*large and influential meeting of ladies and gentlemen*", the acknowledgement by the chairman highlighted that the portrait, by Mr Robert C Crawford (1842–1924), had been three years in planning but suffered delays, not only because of her involvement with the great St Andrews Hall bazaar, but more so due to the recent death of her mother which *"well-nigh prostrated her"*. In her reply, Clugston recalled that when the subject was first raised, that her *"... sainted mother would have been the receiver of the presentation, but God had willed it otherwise"*.[24]

Clugston presented the portrait to Broomhill Home, where it hung for many decades. However, in 1953, the minutes of the Western Regional Hospital Board mention that Messrs T and R Annan of Glasgow were commissioned to trim the full-length painting to a 36 by 28 inch head and shoulders portrait. The painting was then repaired, cleaned and reframed. Rumours persisted that the painting was stolen when the building lay empty, but was recovered at the Barras Market in Glasgow at some time later. The Barras, a street and indoor market in the Calton area of the city, was founded between the war years and has a reputation for selling anything and everything. The painting now lies in the archives of East Dunbartonshire Leisure and Culture Trust.

In 1887 a dispute arose over funds amounting to £3,476 which Clugston had raised at the fundraising bazaar for the establishment of a Fever Hospital in the city in 1866. The Magistrates of Glasgow raised an action at the Court of Session stating that, under the powers of the Public Health (Scotland) Act 1867, those funds should be used for City of Glasgow Fever Hospital which the city had built at Belvidere in 1870, after the closure of the previous Fever Hospital at the Glasgow Royal Infirmary. The Dorcas Society, continuing to work with the patients of the hospital, had already distributed over 5,500 articles of clothing amongst 1,307 convalescent fever patients. On hearing submissions from several interested parties, including a suggestion from Clugston that the money should be split, half to the Dorcas Societies of Belvidere and Govan Fever Hospitals, with the remaining half awarded to the Glasgow Royal Infirmary for the building of a nurses' home. The Court sustained the claim for the Belvidere Dorcas Society, *"with the condition that it must only be applied for the relief of patients within the city. Expenses were given from the funds to all parties"*.[25]

While taking an extended break in the small west coast town of Ardrossan, after retiring to bed in her normal health the previous evening, Clugston was discovered by her housekeeper the following morning, in bed, *"… in the attitude of prayer when the summons came"*.

Beatrice Clugston died at No.3 Arran Place, Ardrossan, on the 4th June 1888 in her 61st year.[26] [27]

In 1891 a memorial by sculptor Mr Pittendrigh MacGillivray was unveiled at the Auld Aisle Cemetery, Kirkintilloch. The memorial, by the head of her grave, designed in the English Gothic Style and standing 13 feet high, featured a cast bronze panel depicting a nurse tending to a patient. Sadly, in 2011 the monument was vandalised with the theft of the bronze panel weighing around 55kg. The panel has never been recovered.[28] [29]

Alice MacKenzie, MBE, a founder member of the Soroptimists of Kirkintilloch and District was the inspiration behind the restoration of the monument. After a lengthy campaign involving Councillor Susan Murray, Soroptimists, Ramblers, Rotary and the Society of Antiquaries, a replacement panel was fitted in 2022.[30]

Sadly, Alice MacKenzie, passed away before the monument was restored. A champion on behalf of women's causes, she was the first librarian for Strathkelvin District Council, a founder of Talking Newspapers, a Rotary Paul Harris Fellow, and she has a shelf dedicated to her in the Glasgow Women's Library. The Paul Harris Fellow is the highest form of recognition a Rotary Club can bestow. Alice was presented with the award for outstanding service to her

Beatrice Clugston Monument. Auld Aisle Cemetery, Kirkintilloch.
Erected 1891. © Jerry Brannigan.

community in appreciation of her 'service above self'.

The Soroptimists, with Cala Homes, planted a tree and plaque in the grounds of Broomhill Home dedicated to Beatrice Clugston, the Soroptimists working with the developers to recognise the heritage and history attached to the site. The housing development was named Beatrice Meadows, with the streets within it referencing some aspect of her life.

It is now also possible to walk with Kirkintilloch Ramblers in the footsteps of Beatrice Clugston from Lenzie Station to Broomhill Home visiting important places in her life.

Some 150 years after its foundation, the Dorcas Charitable Trust continues to provide a variety of services to the Glasgow Royal Infirmary. In 2020 the Trust, in keeping with Clugston's original goal, also administers clothing and basic toiletries, ensuring patients can go home equipped with essentials. From the 1950s, the Trust began the operation of a mobile 'tuck' trolley which visited every ward, giving patients the opportunity to buy sweets and snacks, newspapers and magazines. The Trust is also involved in funding social work projects and the supply of personal appliances for patients in wards, such as television and radio.

To fund all of their goals and projects, the Trust operates a tearoom, Mabel's, on the ground floor of the Glasgow Royal Infirmary.

In 1875 Clugston founded the Association for the Relief of Incurables in Glasgow and the West of Scotland for *"the purpose of establishing and maintaining homes for the relief of persons in Glasgow and West of Scotland suffering from an incurable disease and the aiding of such persons in their own homes."* A proposal for a new constitution, and a new name, the Association for the Relief of Infirmity in the West of Scotland (ARI) was adopted in 2016, with the objective to help those suffering in poverty *"from contracted diseases by awarding one-off grants and monthly grants"*.[31]

Throughout her life, Beatrice Clugston raised upwards of £66,317. A sum which, taking into account inflation to 2020, equates to approximately £8.6m.

The majority of Clugston's hospitals and convalescent homes continued to serve their communities in some form for more than 100 years after her death.

> "*We ought to bless God for such a life as dear as Miss Clugston's – such a work! ... Her works will live after her. ... Excuse a brief note; my thoughts about her are not brief. God bless you and her great institution.*"
>
> Florence Nightingale (August 1888)

References

1 Clugston Family Archive. https://clugstonfamilytree.wordpress.com/home/weavers/

2 1825 McKenzie, Duncan (Old Parish Registers Births 065/Fodderty) Page 27 of 149.

3 1881 Clugston, Mary (Statutory registers Deaths 498/159).

4 Lockhart, Douglas G, *The Queen of all Bazaars, Scottish Local History*, Issue 111. p. 3.

5 1855 Clugston, John (Statutory registers Death 638/1/19).

6 My City Glasgow. www.mycityglasgow.co.uk/index_files/clugston.htm

7 Glasgow Royal Infirmary Dorcas Trust. www.gridorcastrust.org

8 *The Scotsman*, 2nd November 1871, p.2. col. 6.

9 *Glasgow Herald*, 6th November 1871, p. 4. col. 5.

10 *Glasgow Herald*, 15th December 1864, p. 2. col. 6.

11 *Glasgow Convalescent Home, Constitution and by-laws*. https://archive.org/stream/b24921452#page/n13/mode/2up

12 *Glasgow Herald*, 20th December 1866, p. 2. col. 3.

13 *Renfrewshire Independent*, 22nd December 1866, p. 5. col. 2.

14 *Greenock Advertiser*, 26th September 1871, p. 2. col. 4.

15 *Glasgow Herald*, 22nd January 1873, p. 6. col. 1.

16 *Glasgow Herald*, 3rd April 1875, p. 4. col. 5.

17 *Aberdeen and Saltcoats Herald*, 27th February 1875.

18 *Glasgow Herald*, 29th November 1876, p. 5. col. 1.

19 *Ardrossan and Saltcoats Herald*, 2nd December 1876, p. 8. col. 5.

20 *Glasgow Evening Citizen*, 13th May 1880, p. 3. col. 5.

21 *Greenock Telegraph*, 10th September 1880, p. 3. col. 4.

22 *Greenock Telegraph*, 28th February 1882, p. 2. col. 2.

23 *Glasgow Herald*, 8th May 1880, p. 3. col. 5.

24 *Glasgow Herald*, 13th December 1882, p. 10. col. 2.

25 *Evening News and Star*, 16th December 1887, p. 3. col. 4.

26 *Renfrewshire Independent*, 8th June 1888, p. 1. col. 4.

27 *Greenock Telegraph*, 5th June 1888, p. 2. col. 5.

28 *Kirkintilloch Herald*, 23rd December 1891, p. 5. col. 5.

29 *Kirkintilloch Herald*, 9th July 1891, p. 8. col. 1.

30 *Mapping Memorials to Women in Scotland.* https://www.womenofscotland.org.uk

31 *Association for the Relief of Infirmity in the West of Scotland.* https://www.ariws.scot

John Rae.
Stromness, Orkney.
Image © Anna Gudge

John Rae

JOHN Rae was born at the Hall of Clestrain, near Stromness in the Orkney Islands, on 30th September 1813. He was of nine children, to John Rae, an Orcadian, and his wife Margaret Glen Campbell of Argyle. John Rae Senior worked as the estate factor for Lord Armadale, Lord Advocate, who lived in Edinburgh.[1]

Rae's childhood upbringing prepared him for a life of adventure; he was home-tutored with his free time spent hunting, fishing and sailing, before he left the island in 1829 to study medicine in Edinburgh, qualifying as a doctor in April 1833.

His father was also the Orkney agent for the Hudson's Bay Company. Orkney was situated in a strategically important location for ships beginning their travels northwards, as the islands were the last port of call where fresh water and supplies could be taken on board. These ships were a vital source of employment for the men of Orkney. The cold and often harsh conditions they had grown up with made them ideally suited for work in the Arctic. Two of Rae's brothers had already joined the company before Rae himself accepted a post as doctor on the Hudson's Bay Company's ship, *Prince of Wales*, two months after his graduation.[2]

The *Prince of Wales* became locked in by ice, forcing Rae to winter in Canada, and it seemed a natural progression when he accepted the position as surgeon and clerk at Moose Factory, the Hudson's Bay Company post on James Bay. Rae spent ten years here not only tending to the company's employees but also to the native Cree Indians. He is quoted as saying this was a "*very happy home for me for ten years*". It was here, living and working with the Cree people, where he learned the survival skills he would later call upon in his Arctic explorations. Not only did he dress in caribou clothing, Rae soon became accomplished at fishing and hunting Arctic animals, and, most crucially, he mastered how to construct an igloo.[3]

It was a condition of the Hudson's Bay Company's licence that surveying the coastline was part of their normal working routine and Rae was tasked with completion of the survey of the northern coastline of North America. In the past, fur traders Samuel Hearne, Sir Alexander MacKenzie, Peter Dease and Thomas Simpson had completed sections, while naval parties led by Sir John Franklin and others had added to this knowledge. But first, he had to be trained to use surveying equipment; to do this, he made an astonishing 1200-mile walk on snowshoes to reach the isolated village of his tutor.[4]

Where expeditions by others involved dozens, sometimes hundreds of men, Rae believed in travelling with as few in the undertaking as absolutely necessary. He began the survey taking 10 men, with a local Inuit interpreter and his son, carrying a small amount of food and living off the land as they moved.[5]

The party travelled in two small boats, transferring to sledges and snowshoes when the ice closed in and made sea travel impossible. Winter quarters were established in Repulse Bay where accommodation, storehouses for the game they shot, and two magnetic observatories were built. In 1847 the party reached the east coast of the Boothia Peninsula, connecting the survey with that of Sir John and Sir James Clark Ross. They then continued to explore the west coast of the Melville Peninsula, almost reaching the area explored by Sir William Edward Parry in 1821. Rae discovered that Boothia was a peninsula and not an island as had been previously thought.

This expedition was important, not only for geographical and meteorological results, but because John Rae had shown that he could lead a successful expedition into the Arctic and survive an Arctic winter by primarily living off the land.

The following year, 1848, Sir John Richardson requested Rae's assistance in the search for the missing expedition of Sir John Franklin,

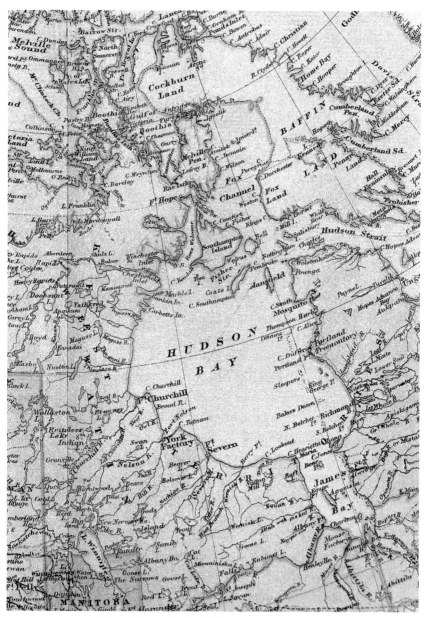

Map of Canada detail, featuring Hudson Bay.
From Bacon's Geographical Establishment Map of Canada. 1908.

which had set out to find the Northwest Passage – the final part of a navigable route from the Atlantic to the Arctic Ocean. Two ships, HMS Erebus and HMS Terror, crewed by 128 officers and men, set sail from England on 19th May 1845.

Franklin was no stranger to the harsh Arctic conditions. His first expedition in 1819, with 20 men tracking the coastline by land, almost ended in complete disaster. A shortage of supplies forced Franklin to abandon the expedition. They then decided to split into groups to try to reach Fort Enterprise, where Franklin expected to find fresh supplies.[6]

Robert Hood, who had been too ill to travel, along with Richardson and Hepburn, remained at the base. Franklin led a group towards Fort Enterprise, while a group led by George Black set out to search for Inuit, who had previously supplied the expedition with food.

Four of Franklin's party found the going too difficult and attempted to return to the base. Of the four, only one survived the journey, Michael Teroahaute. Teroahaute had also arrived bearing fresh meat, leading Richardson to conclude that the source of this meat could only be the flesh of Teroahaute's lost companions.

A few days later, when Teroahaute and Hood were alone, a shot rang out and Hood was found with a bullet wound to his head. Teroahaute claimed that Hood had committed suicide.

The three who remained at base, Teroahaute, Richardson and Hepburn, decided to head for Franklin and Fort Enterprise, but on the way, convinced they would be murdered by the flesh-eating monster in their midst, Richardson took responsibility as the senior officer, and shot Teroahaute dead.

Richardson and Hepburn arrived at Fort Enterprise to find there were no fresh supplies, with those remaining having resorted to drinking a soup made of lichen and boiled boot leather in an effort to survive. Remarkably, the group led by George Black did find Inuit, who then travelled to Fort Enterprise to the rescue of the malnourished men. On the verge of death, Franklin himself was fortunate to live. Of the 20 men who started out the survey, only nine survived.

To lose more than half of the expedition would seem to be a failure but, somehow, the Royal Navy, aided by triumphalist newspaper headlines, turned the story around, hailing Franklin as "*The man who ate his boots*". The public were enthralled by stories of Franklin's apparent bravery, acclaiming him as a national hero.

When Rae was tasked with searching for the missing expedition 26 years later, neither the Royal Navy nor Sir John Franklin appeared to have learned any lessons from his first Arctic catastrophe.

There had been no trace of the men or ships since the summer of 1845, a gap of three years, which resulted in the British government offering a reward of £10,000 for news of their fate.[7] Richardson, Rae and the party made an extremely arduous canoe journey from Toronto to the mouth of the Mackenzie River on the edge of the Arctic Ocean in 96 days. Ice hampered the search, forcing them to winter on Great Bear Lake. Richardson returned to England while Rae continued making the journey down the Coppermine River to the Arctic Ocean. He explored the Rae River, named after him by Richardson the previous year, but again ice forced him to abandon the search, returning to Fort Simpson where, in his absence, he had been promoted to Chief Trader.[8]

The position of Chief Trader didn't suit Rae. He was unaccustomed to the world of accountancy and business management, leading to his promotion as Chief Factor in 1850, with responsibility for the Mackenzie River area. This allowed him freedom to travel while continuing to carry out surveys of the coastline. Looking for traces of Franklin's expedition became part of his day-to-day life; future sailings consisted of both surveying and searching for signs of the missing men and ships.

In the winter of 1850, he resumed his search for Franklin at the request of the Admiralty, leaving Fort Confidence in 1851 with two boats he had built and rigged to his own specification; crossing over the ice with men, sledges and dogs. Moving eastward along the coast, he found no strait dividing Wollaston Land from Victoria Land, linking his own findings with those of Dease and Simpson in 1839. The party reached Kendall River, having covered 824 miles in 42 days.

In a letter to Sir George Simpson, Governor-in-Chief of the Hudson's Bay Company's Territories, sent from the Kendall River Provision Station on 10th June 1851, Rae details his 42 days exploration of the coast from 25th April to 10th June.

In the letter, he gives some detail of the coastline he and his men covered, with names of the land surveyed. Sir John Richardson, Wellbank, Simpson, Colvile, Pullen, Bell, Baring and Sir George Black were some of the names listed. In the journey they built 'snow houses' and 'snow walls' as they camped and hunted for food as required. Rae notes their regular food hunted as geese, partridges and lemmings, and also rabbits and deer. On one occasion a 'ground bear' had found and destroyed a cache, then followed them for some time, before leaving the area. They only hunted when provisions were low or needed to stock up on a cache of food to be left in the snow. Rae's small group met *'Esquimaux'* several times but there was no trace of the Franklin expedition.[9]

In April 1852, the Royal Geographical Society awarded Rae the Founder's Gold Medal for his discoveries of 1846–47 and 1851. He used the publicity generated to propose a further expedition to the Hudson's Bay Company to complete the survey.

In the two newly constructed boats, Rae left with a party of 11, sailing for Victoria Island, exploring and surveying as they travelled. Walking on the rough ice meant that footwear wore out quickly, leaving *"… every footstep marked with blood"*. Rae found two pieces of machined wood which most likely came from one of Franklin's ships and, with the threat of the ice pack closing in on them again, he brought these pieces back to England. This may have been a highly successful expedition, but the fate of Franklin remained unsolved.

Made leader of the new expedition in June 1852, Rae and the

party immediately began their work. In the spring, Rae travelled in sledges with four men to Pella Bay, where he met an Inuit who told him that a party of at least 35–40 'Kabloonans' had starved to death west of a "… *large river a long way off*". This was the first firm piece of news of the fate of the Franklin expedition.

Rae bought a cap band from the Inuit. He had not seen the dead bodies himself, nor could he place the position on a chart. Thinking the information too vague to act upon, Rae continued the survey, reaching their destination of Repulse Bay on 26th May 1853, where the party overwintered. In 1854, Rae received more news of the Franklin expedition from the Inuit, buying artefacts from the Erebus and Terror and hearing stories of a group of some 40 white men on King William Land dragging a boat and sledges to the south.

Later accounts spoke of the bodies of around 30 men scattered around graves on the mainland; in addition, there were said to be five bodies on an island. Rae immediately made preparations to return to England with the first news of Franklin and his men.[10]

Geographically, his discovery that King William Land was an island, separated from the Boothia Peninsula by a strait (later named the Rae Strait) was important. Through this 14-mile-wide Rae Strait, he had charted the location of the final part of the long sought-after Northwest Passage, the sea route connecting the Atlantic and Pacific Oceans through the Arctic Archipelago of Canada.

When Rae arrived in London on Sunday 22nd October 1854, his news caused a sensation. His report to the Admiralty was leaked to *The Times*; publication followed the next day and caused outrage.

The Times of Monday, October 23rd 1865 reported:

"The bodies of some thirty persons were discovered. Some were in a tent, others under a boat which had been turned to form a shelter. From the mutilated state of many of the corpses and from the contents of the kettles it is evident that our wretched countrymen had been driven to the 'last resource', cannibalism as a means of prolonging existence."

In a report from 2014 by the Royal Canadian Geographical Society, Franklin's fate is explained. After the first winter frozen in the ice, they became free, sailing, or moving with the ice 300 miles south before the sea froze around them again. During this period, before the sea froze over once more, Captain John Franklin died on 11th June 1847. After their third winter trapped in the ice, with supplies failing, the surviving crew abandoned the ships on 22nd April 1848, and attempted to march several hundred miles to the south of King William Land and the nearest trading post. They had no way of knowing that King William Land was an island.

The men set off dragging boats laden with equipment and supplies, some pushing, some pulling, over the snow and ice. It would have been an energy-sapping, dispiriting, and agonisingly slow ordeal for them. An Inuit story is told of a meeting between the men with their boat and two Inuit hunters in the Arctic wilderness. The Inuit spoke of the men being tired and starving, but having no English, a conversation wasn't possible. They did give the men some of their food but recognised that their own meagre rations would be nowhere near enough to sustain them.

John Franklin, and 24 of his officers and men, had died by April 1848 when the decision was made to abandon the ships. The remaining officers and crew set out on foot to try to reach safety. Not a single one of Franklin's crew of 129 survived.[11]

A shocked London society simply refused to believe that men of the Royal Navy could have resorted to cannibalism. Charles Dickens wrote that men of the Royal Navy "… *would or could not in any extremity of hunger, alleviate pains of starvation by this horrible means*". Newspapers then criticised Rae for not having verified the reports himself, suggesting he was too busy hurrying home to claim the £10,000 reward. Rae insisted he knew nothing of such a reward until he returned to England, and, standing by his report, he refused to be dragged into outrageous newspaper allegations. Author Ken

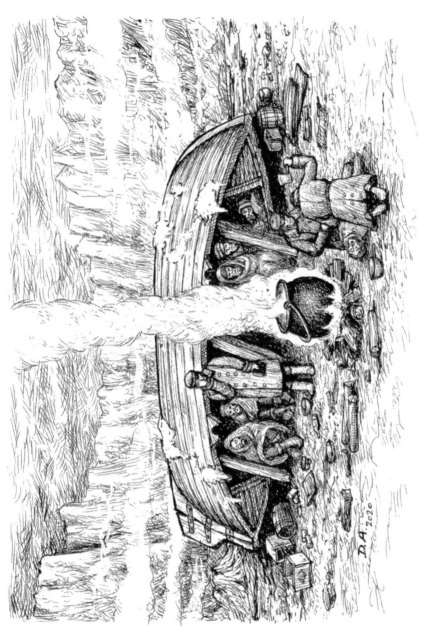

The Fate of the Franklin Crew. © David Alexander

McGoogan writes it would not have been possible for Rae to travel, or to begin to search with the distinct probability of being trapped in the ice for another season. [12]

Two years later, an expedition by Sir Leopold McClintock visited the gruesome site and largely confirmed Rae's findings. It wasn't until that point that John Rae received the £10,000 reward money.

Lady Jane Franklin, Sir John Franklin's widow, refused to allow her late husband's name and legacy to be tarnished and set about using all her resources and contacts to bring James Rae's reputation into disrepute. She had previously pressured the Admiralty to send search ships when nothing was heard from the expedition. She used her own fortune to finance five search ships, indeed at one point there were 15 ships in the area searching for Franklin. In 1860, for her contribution to Arctic research, Lady Jane Franklin became the first woman to be awarded the Royal Geographical Society's Founder Medal.[13]

Her friend, author Charles Dickens, joined her campaign and wrote several articles demonising Rae and the Inuit. Dickens suggested that savages had murdered the starving men. In one of his articles, he writes of the Inuit, "... *the chatter of a gross handful of uncivilised people, with a domesticity of blood and blubber*".[14] [15]

Lady Franklin, determined that her husband's failures be recognised as successes and to see him immortalised as a Royal Navy hero, campaigned tirelessly for a statue to be commissioned in his memory. Subsequently, a statue was erected in Waterloo Place (not her preferred site of Trafalgar Square). She followed this by commissioning a large monumental bust which was placed in Westminster Abbey, claiming that he had discovered the Northwest Passage. Alongside, a panel read, "*Died June 11. 1847, off Point Victory in the frozen ocean. The beloved chief of the gallant crews who perished with him in completing the discovery of the north-west passage.*"

Lady Franklin's concerted efforts to remove John Rae's name from the history of Arctic exploration proved to be largely successful. The constantly negative publicity generated by Lady Franklin ensured that John Rae was never offered a knighthood. He was the only Arctic explorer of the time not to be honoured in this way.

Between 1846 and 1854, John Rae led four expeditions to the Arctic, travelling over 10,000 miles on foot, sledges, or in small boats, surveying some 1,800 miles of coastline. In the course of his travels, he discovered features now known as the Rae Peninsula and the Rae River.

Rae retired in 1856. In 1857, as a shareholder, he appeared on behalf of the Hudson's Bay Company before a select committee in the House of Commons in London convened to investigate the company's activities.

In January 1860, he married Catherine Jane Alicia (Kate) in Toronto, the third child of Major George Ash Thomson of Londonderry. The Raes made their home in Britain, and in the same year he took part in surveying the route of the transatlantic cable which was laid via Scotland, the Faroe Islands, Iceland and Greenland.

In his retirement, Dr John Rae divided his last years between London and Orkney. He was a familiar figure in Kirkwall and well-known to the town's people. He indulged in hunting and sailing, his two favourite hobbies from childhood, and kept a pony for visits to the moors. On his own small yacht, he took part in the annual Kirkwall regatta, winning the first prize on at least one occasion.[16]

Dr John Rae F.R.S., F.R.G.S. died in his London home at 4 Addison Gardens, Kensington of a ruptured aneurysm on 22 July 1893, age 80. He is buried in the churchyard of St Magnus Cathedral, Kirkwall, Orkney, where a memorial was erected by public subscription in 1895. His effigy wears Arctic clothes, his gun by his side. [17]

In November of the same year, his widow presented her late husband's collection of Arctic and 'other curiosities' to the University of Edinburgh.[18] [19]

For his work in the field, he was awarded an honorary doctorate degree by McGill University, Montreal in 1853.

Rae was made a member of the Royal Scottish Geographical

Map of Canada detail, featuring King William Land and Rae Straight.
From Bacon's Geographical Establishment Map of Canada. 1908.

Society from 1885, and in 1866 Edinburgh University made him an honorary Doctor of Law.

On Monday 29th December 1896 a memorial was unveiled at Kirkwall Cathedral. A large gathering was present to hear an account of the exploits of Rae.[20]

Between 1903 and 1906, 50 years after Rae charted the channel, explorer Roald Amundsen led the first expedition to cross the Northwest Passage between the Atlantic and Pacific Oceans. However, while Amundsen became the first man to navigate the route, it had no practical worth as the journey took three years, using a shallow draft boat forced to follow the coastline when not locked in by ice.[21]

In 1992 Professor Anne Keenleyside, bioarchaeologist from Trent University, examined a second camp in the fatal Franklin expedition. The group found bones scattered over the site and, after forensic examination, determined that cut marks found on the bones were not of animal origin. They were made by a metal blade.[22]

In 1993, in recognition of his achievements, the centenary of Rae's death was marked with an exhibition by the National Museums of Scotland in association with Tankerhouse Museum, Kirkwall. The exhibition ran for five months in Edinburgh, followed by five months in Orkney. This was the first time that Rae's life had been recognised outside of Orkney.[23]

In more recent times, Rae has attracted admirers such as Vilhjalmur Stefansson, Arctic explorer and ethnologist, not only for his discoveries, but for Rae's ability to live off the land, recognising him as the leader in the field of Arctic survival.

Rae Mears, an authority on the subject of bushcraft and survival, stated in 2009, "*In my opinion, he was the greatest Arctic explorer ever, the man who succeeded where others had failed.... He had learned to live there as though it was his home. ... Rae does not deserve to be brushed aside. His achievements were astounding. He undertook four Arctic expeditions with the loss of one life, he mapped around 1.5 thousand miles*

John Rae and Clestrain. Image ©James Grieve

of coastline, he found the Franklin Expedition and he discovered the Rae Strait, the final link to the Northwest Passage."[24]

Dr John Rae. His life and Legacy, was the subject of a major international conference in Orkney in 2013, the bicentenary of his birth. A statue of the Arctic explorer by local sculptor Ian Scott was unveiled at Stromness Pierhead during the event.[25]

It wasn't until 2014 when a plaque was unveiled in Westminster Abbey recognising John Rae's work. It is a simple floor plaque inscribed only, *"John Rae, Arctic Explorer"*.[26]

In the early to mid-1800s, the ice was frozen in places to a depth of 10 metres, trapping many ships and men for several Arctic winters and taking many lives. In the 21st century, with the effects of global warming, there is much less ice, and for longer periods, resulting in routes through the Canadian Arctic Archipelago which are open to deep draft ships, such as tankers and military vessels, for several months of the year.[27]

John Rae

A dispute claiming that the channels be classified as international waters and open to all ships from all countries has now arisen, underlining the importance of the work by John Rae.

References

1 The John Rae Society. *John Rae Biography.* www.johnraesociety.com/john-rae/
2 Orkneyjar, *Dr John Rae – The Unsung Arctic Hero.* https://orkneyjar.com/history/historicalfigures/johnrae
3 *Undiscovered Scotland.* https://www.undiscoveredscotland.co.uk/usbiography/r/johnrae.html
4 *Undiscovered Scotland.* 1,200 miles on snowshoes.
5 *Oxford Dictionary of National Biography* (ODNB), Savours, Ann, 2004.
6 *Britain's Small Forgotten Wars.* The Franklin Coppermine Expedition, 1819–22.
7 *Undiscovered Scotland.* https://www.undiscoveredscotland.co.uk/usbiography/r/johnrae.html.
8 *Evening Mail*, 2nd January 1850, p. 3. col. 2.
9 *Daily News (London)*, 11th November 1851, pp. 5–6.
10 *The Orkney Herald*, 12th July 1933, p. 3. col. 5–7. p. 6 col. 4–5.
11 *Undiscovered Scotland.* Confirmation.
12 Edinburgh Lecture for the Royal Society of Edinburgh. *John Rae* by Ken McGoogan. 22nd April 2013. https://www.youtube.com/watch?v=9UUjQz1BSgA
13 Orkneyjar, *Dr John Rae – The Unsung Arctic Hero.* https://orkneyjar.com/history/historicalfigures/johnrae
14 *National Post*, 27th October 2016, Tristin Hopper, article.
15 *CBS News*, 5th May 2008. Article. Apology by Dickens Descendant.
16 *Orkney Herald*, 17th June 1942, p. 8. Col. 3.
17 *Wellington Journal*, 29th July 1893, p. 2. Col. 6.
18 *Orkney Herald*, 2nd April 1930, p 8. col. 1–3.
19 *Aberdeen Evening Express*, 6th November 1893, p. 2. col. 5.
20 *Dundee Courier*, 1st January 1896, p 4. col. 3.
21 Edinburgh Lecture for the Royal Society of Edinburgh. *John Rae* by Ken McGoogan. 22nd April 2013.
22 Professor Anne Keenleyside. Trent University. https://www.researchgate.net/scientific-contributions/Anne-Keenleyside-72601371
23 *Aberdeen Press and Journal*, 28th August 1992, p. 35. col. 3.
24 Rae Mears, *Northern Wilderness.* S1 Ep 4. BBC Productions, 2009. https://www.youtube.com/watch?v=Q4EbbH5mZzU
25 *The Orcadian*, 28th September 2013. 3-Day Conference.
26 *Westminster Abbey.* John Rae biography. https://www.westminster-abbey.org/abbey-commemorations/commemorations/dr-john-rae/
27 University of Massachusetts Amherst. *History of sea ice in the Arctic.* www.geo.umass.edu

Teenage Rose Reilly practicing on the public playing fields at Stewarton.
Image with the permission of Rose Reilly.

Rose Reilly

ROSE Reilly was born in Stewarton, East Ayrshire on 2nd January 1955. Based in Ayr during the war, her father, Hugh Reilly, from Plains in Airdrie, met his wife-to-be, Bridget Lynch, a nurse working in Ailsa Hospital on the outskirts of the town.[1]

The Reillys are a large family of three boys and five girls, including two sets of twins. Rose has a twin sister Mary.

At age three, in one of Reilly's earliest memories, she recalls being given a doll for Christmas but, in a tantrum, threw it away. She wasn't interested in 'girlie' things and got what she wanted in the end by swapping the doll for a ball. That ball went everywhere with her, including her bed, as she was frightened her mother would come and take it while she was sleeping. Even now, Reilly can't remember a time in her life when she wanted to do anything other than play football.

Growing up in Stewarton, a small town around five miles from Kilmarnock, opportunities to play football in an organised team were non-existent for young girls. When she was seven, Reilly approached the coach of Stewarton United Boys Club and told him she wanted to play for his team. He took little persuading; living in a small town, he was very well aware of her skills and welcomed her, but only on the condition she had her hair cut. Girls weren't allowed in his team; however, he would bend the rules if they could pretend she was a boy. An overjoyed Reilly at once went to the local barber and had her hair cut short, insisting to the hesitant barber that her mother knew but couldn't come down herself. When her irate mother saw the haircut, she went straight to the barber's shop. Reilly later said she was surprised she didn't hear her mother tear strips off the barber from her house. However, it was a fait accompli:

she had her short hair, she could play proper football, and it didn't matter that her new football name was Ross.[2]

It didn't take long before other coaches noticed her skills. A scout from Celtic Football Club was present at one match when Reilly was once again outstanding, scoring seven goals. He was astonished to discover the "*wee number seven guy*" who caught his interest was a girl.[3]

As she got older, Reilly set her sights on playing for the local ladies' team, Stewarton Thistle Ladies, and approached their coach and organiser, Elsie Cook. Cook looked at the seemingly delicate girl standing in front of her and, thinking her too young and too small, suggested she should come back in two years. Reilly spent those two years working on her strength and skills and, exactly two years to the day from her first refusal, approached Cook again, boots under her arms, and was accepted into the team. It was immediately obvious she was no ordinary girl, and with her skills and abilities, Reilly quickly became a regular player at Stewarton Thistle. The 10-year-old Reilly was by far the youngest player on the field.

Those two years working on her physical development led Reilly into athletics, but devoting all her time to a combination of football and athletics meant, with attendance best described as erratic, her schoolwork suffered. So much so that when she was 15, the headmaster of her secondary school suggested she need not come back after the summer holidays. Her usual determination ensured success, being selected for the Scotland training squad for the 1970 Commonwealth Games, as a 16-year-old pentathlete. When the pair met at a function in Reilly's honour many years later, he admitted it was a suggestion he had come to regret.

The combination of playing regular football and her serious interest in athletics couldn't continue. It came to a head when her athletics coach advised Reilly that by playing football, she was developing muscles in her thighs, using the term 'fitba thighs'. The news stunned

Rose Reilly displaying the strength and determination
that typified her desire to become a professional football player.
Image with the permission of Rose Reilly.

Reilly; she loved the variation and personal pressure of the athletics field and decided to take a break from football. The break lasted only one week. Fitba thighs or not, the pull of the football pitch was too strong. Her parents were devastated; they could already see the progress she had made as an athlete, but they could see no future for their daughter as a football player.[4]

Stewarton Thistle, with 15-year-old Reilly at the front, won the inaugural Scottish Women's Cup in season 1970–71. That same season, they reached the final of the FA Cup in England, losing 4–1 to Southampton, who were to become their nemesis in this tournament. Played under the auspices of the English Women's Football Association, which admitted teams from Scotland and Wales in its formative years, 71 teams took part in the competition. Playing under the name of Lee's Ladies because of a club sponsorship deal, they again reached the final in 1972, once more against Southampton. Again, the English team lifted the trophy, winning 3–2.

In 1972 Reilly moved to Westthorn United Ladies Football Club, and in 1973 Westthorn also reached the final of the FA Cup, yet again meeting Southampton, who captured the cup, winning 2–0.

Women's football wasn't new; Mary Queen of Scots is said to have owned the oldest football in existence, and women's football in England was mentioned in a poem of 1580. In Scotland, church records from Carstairs reference women playing football in 1629.

As men's football was highly successful, in 1881, a group of theatre entrepreneurs devised a scheme to tour Scotland v England women's internationals throughout the length and breadth of the country.

The first advertised match of this tour, becoming the first advertised women's international in the world, took place on 10th May 1881, at the Easter Road ground in Edinburgh. This, however, wasn't football as we know it today. It appears that one team was made up primarily of dancers and the other of actresses and singers, with little regard for the nationality of the players who comprised each team.[5]

Lily St Clair scored Scotland's first goal in a 3–0 victory over England. Researcher Stuart Gibbs and local history researcher, Jane Roberts, have indicated that Lily St Clair is thought to have been music hall actress Lillian Davis.

On 16th May 1881, a second match in Glasgow's Shawfield Stadium attracted a crowd of 5,000 spectators, but by half-time the crowd was openly disturbed by the lack of any football knowledge, tactical, or positional awareness being shown on the pitch. Hundreds invaded the field, leading to a clash with police and an early escape from Glasgow by the players and organisers. The majority of further games on the tour brought similar complaints, with matches also being brought to a halt by field invasions of irate supporters.

During the First World War, men had been sent to war while women were left to take their places in the factories; they also took their places on the football fields. What was new were the crowds, and these large attendances at women's football were seen as a danger to the men's game. In 1928 the Scottish Football Association (SFA) declined to give permission for women to take part in any league or competition which came under their control. The men of the SFA felt that women's bodies were not capable of withstanding the rigours of football.

After World War II, they maintained their control, with government and football authorities keen to see women return to their domestic roles.

In Europe, particularly in France and Italy, women's football grew and flourished, while in Scotland the SFA continued to put constant obstacles in their way in an attempt to stop any development in the women's game. They refused permission for women to use any facilities, pitches, or equipment which came under control of the association. Crucially, they also withheld the use of officials and referees.

On 18th November 1972, Reilly played in the first ever official Scotland v England women's international, which took place at Ravenscraig Stadium, Greenock, in front of "... *an enthusiastic crowd of about 400*". Reilly scored direct from a corner, but England snatched a late winner in the 3–2 thriller.[6]

It wasn't until 1974, under pressure from the International Federation of Association Football (FIFA) and the Union of European Football Associations (UEFA), women's movements, and government, that the SFA tacitly admitted to the existence of women's football. However, as there were no leagues or competitions affiliated with the governing body, women with aspirations to make any sort of career from the sport were forced to leave the country.

At 17, Reilly decided the time had come to turn professional but she had no idea how to go about it. As an avid reader of the sports pages, she thought to approach the then sports editor of the *Daily Record*, Stan Chivas, for advice. She made the bus journey to the *Record's* Glasgow office, told the receptionist she had an appointment with Mr Chivas, and five minutes later she was talking to him. Her showing up in his office came as more than a surprise, with Reilly commenting, "*He looked at me as if I was crazy.*" Chivas took her seriously, and two weeks later his newspaper sponsored a trip to France for a specially arranged trial match with professional women's team Stade de Reims. Reilly persuaded her Stewarton teammate Edna Neillis to join the adventure, and the pair set off. It was Neillis who insisted "*we don't do trials*". Sure enough, at the end of the first 45 minutes, the pair were offered contracts.[7]

They were at Reims for only four months before AC Milan arrived to offer both girls contracts. It was a no-brainer for Reilly; as she put it, "*They play their games in the San Siro, you don't say no to that.*" When she arrived at the San Siro, Reilly walked over every part of the pitch, savouring every moment. She stood in the wings, imagining herself beating defenders before crossing the ball into the goal, visualising a striker leaping to head it into the net. She walked to one goalmouth, picturing herself getting the final touch, slipping the ball over the goal line. Then she walked the length of the park, as if walking through a game in progress, repeating the process in the other goalmouth. In her mind, she took ownership of the pitch, undaunted of a return as a player.[8]

Unfortunately, Edna Neillis suffered badly from homesickness and returned to Scotland shortly after arriving in Milan.[9]

Determined to make a success of the move, Reilly trained on her own under the midday sun when the others were resting, and then did it all again when the team trained later in the day. This strength of willpower saw her become Scotland's first full-time professional female football player.

AC Milan booked her into a hotel, close to the training ground in

Lake Como, for what became a full year. As she made her daily walk to the training ground, Reilly decided that if she was going to get anywhere in her new surroundings, she needed to speak the language. She bought the Italian sports newspaper, *La Gazzetta dello Sport*, and using an Italian–English dictionary, learned three new words every day. As she recalled with her usual self-deprecation, she felt "*... four words would be too many for her uneducated brain*".

She tried to translate the sports stories, then on her walk to training she would stop and make an effort to talk to locals. Soon, she became a familiar figure, engaging in conversations which slowly became more fluent. With her ability to speak to the media and teammates in their own language, Reilly quickly felt at home, falling in love with the country and its people. The Italian people returned the compliment.[10]

In 1975, shortly after Reilly signed for AC Milan, the SFA took great exception to a newspaper article given to *The Sunday People*, which reported Reilly, Elsie Cook and Edna Neillis' criticism of the SFA's method of appointing the new women's Scottish national team manager, Bill Cranston. On January 25th 1975 at a meeting in Edinburgh, Neillis and Cook arrived to defend themselves but were so outraged at the treatment they received, they walked out. Reilly, in Italy, received no notice and had no idea that proceedings were even happening. In the absence of all three women, the SFA handed down the most Draconian sentences in their power: they were suspended, sine die, "*... the stiffest ever sentence imposed on women in this country – indefinite suspension*". Elsie Cook, a former Scottish women's team manager herself, had her honorary membership of the Scottish Football Association – which she helped found – withdrawn. Charles Leggett, vice-chairman of the SFA, said, "*It is true the girls were banned because they talked to The Sunday People. They seem to want to do all the talking because they have now gone to a solicitor.*" Later, when Reilly heard the decision, she commented, "*Talking to The Sunday People* *isn't a crime when we are praising them, but they are not big enough to take criticism."* [11]

The sine die verdict meant Reilly, still only 17, would never add to the 10 Scottish caps already awarded. However, the Italian authorities were quick to see the possibilities, particularly as there were no Europe-wide governing bodies to legislate eligibility. As Reilly describes, they found a creative answer by offering dual nationality. *"The AC Milan President asked me if I would play for Italy with Italian citizenship. Of course, I accepted; it was a great honour for me. That's how my career started with the Italian jersey; as I've said, there was always a Scottish heart beating under an Italian jersey."*

When the governing bodies, FIFA and UEFA, took over the running of women's football, they introduced eligibility rules, forcing Reilly's club management to find an imaginative solution to the problem. The Italian Federation were so desperate to keep her, they suggested arranging for her to marry an elderly gent in a care home, thereby securing citizenship. It was an offer Reilly could turn down, citing her Catholic upbringing, but the real reason may have been the expected wrath of her mother: *"She would have bloody killed me!"* Many years later, she joked, *"... see if he was a millionaire, I should have done it"*.

In 1981, when Reilly played for Lecce, she answered a call for help from her first foreign club, Reims, in France. As Reilly put it, *"I would play with Lecce on a Saturday afternoon and then fly to Paris to play on Sunday for Reims. We won both championships. ... I was always myself, with my bag over the shoulder. Just me and the game."*

After a post-match meal with Lecce, Reilly was struck down with food poisoning, suddenly becoming very ill. Her condition quickly deteriorated, forcing her transfer into critical care. Reilly recounts how hepatitis had *"... taken over my body, I was weak, very weak, I couldn't stand up"*, and when warned that her football career might be over her reply was, *"... well you would be as well killing me here then"*.

Reilly holds aloft the Mundialito Femminile. 1984.
Image with the permission of Rose Reilly.

On her release from hospital, with her usual iron determination, Reilly vowed to play again even though she struggled to stand up for any length of time. Fifty yards a day was her self-imposed target: a simple walk from her home to the training ground and back again. Once fulfilled, she ran the 50 yards there and back. It took time, but she not only made it back onto the pitch, a short time later Reilly was voted the world's best female player.[12] [13]

In 1984 Reilly led the forward line of the Italian team that won the *Mundialito Femminile*, the precursor to the Women's World Cup. The competition took place in Italy; the final played out in Livorno at the Armando Picchi Stadium on 26th August, seeing Italy victorious against West Germany with a final score of 3–1. The first goal came from a cross by Reilly, then Reilly herself scored the second; a typical striker's goal, pouncing in the six-yard area after a goalmouth scramble (19 min). A penalty before half-time ensured a comfortable second half, with West Germany scoring a consolation goal. Reilly was voted the player of the tournament.[14]

The following October, the Italian team took part in the Xi'an Women's Tournament in Beijing, playing against several Chinese teams along with the national teams from Japan and Australia. Beaten in the semi-final, the Italian team won third place with a 5–1 win over Japan. The top scorer with ten goals in the four matches, Reilly was named the best female footballer in the world.[15]

Reilly was one of the top players in a league where money was king. When a transfer was set up, the players were pawns and had to go where they were sent. The clubs had all the power – just as they did in the men's game. During her time in Italy, Reilly played for nine teams, AC Milan, Catania, Lecce, Napoli, Fiorentina, Prato, Agilani, Bari, and Trani.

In a long football career, Reilly was a winner in the inaugural Scottish Women's Cup Final in season 1970–71, and in the same season was a losing finalist in the Football Association FA Cup. In the following two seasons, 1971–72 and 1972–73, Riley was again a losing FA Cup finalist. In France, she won a league winner's medal with Stade de Reims, and in Italy she won eight league winner's medals and four cups finals.

She won 2 Golden Boot awards with Catania and Lecce; to add to the 10 international caps won with the Scottish national team, she played 22 times for Italy. In 1984, Reilly became the first, and to date the only, Scot to have won the Mundialito Femminile, the Women's World Cup. Shortly after her World Cup victory, at the Xi'n International Tournament in China, Reilly was voted the world's best player.

On her retirement from the professional game, Reilly settled in Bari, opening a sports shop in nearby Trani. However, football was forever in her blood and she talked her way into playing for a team of local policemen. More than able to hold her own with the men, only a torn calf muscle forced her retirement from the game at age 40. The injury proved fortuitous as she was treated by local physiotherapist, Norberto Peralta, an Argentine who had started a practice in Bari. They married on Christmas Eve, 1998, with only two witnesses present. Two years later, at the age of 45, Reilly gave birth to daughter, Valentina.[16]

Reilly returned home in the same year to introduce her newborn daughter to her mother, only to be called back a few months later when her mother suffered a severe stroke. *"I always had an up and down relationship with my mother but when something like this happens, it's all about family,"* Reilly said. Critically ill, the doctors gave her little time but, with family care, she survived a further nine years.

Reilly, now settled with Valentina and Norberto in Scotland, continues to visit friends and holiday in Italy.

She was a familiar face in football-loving Italy; however, in Scotland, with the exception of Stewarton, she remained unknown until, in March 2007, she was inducted into the Scottish Sports Hall of Fame, established in 2002 by Sport Scotland, Scotland's national agency for sport, to recognise and honour the great champions the country has produced.

In November 2007, she became the first woman inducted into the Scottish Football Hall of Fame. It took the Scottish Football Association 11 more years to find another woman who was, in their view, worthy of a place in the SFA Hall of Fame. Currently, Rose Reilly and Julie Fleeting MBE remain the only female inductees.[17]

On 7th January 1987, BBC1 screened a documentary, *Home and Away* about the fortunes of Reilly and the English footballer Kerry Davis who were both playing their football in Italy.[18] [19] [20]

"I was used to getting awards in Italy because that's where my career was. I didn't expect to be recognised here in Scotland. It was a proud moment to be accepted into the Hall of Fame and I hope I've opened the door for more female footballers."[21]

In 2011 she was the first woman to receive the Professional Footballers' Association Scotland Special Merit Award.

On 1st December 2015, she was awarded an Honorary Doctorate from the University of the West of Scotland.[22]

On 28th May 2019, in front of a record crowd of 18,555 in Glasgow, when Scotland's Women beat Jamaica 3–2 in a friendly match, Scotland's First Minister Nicola Sturgeon presented Reilly, Margaret McAulay, Linda Kidd and Jean Stewart the Scottish international caps they had been denied for playing for their country. Awarding a footballer a 'cap' dates back to the early days of the sport when players would wear caps during the game. A player being chosen to play for their home international team is said to have earned a 'cap', with the single physical cap awarded representing all the games that player may have played for their country.[23]

In June 2019, a documentary titled *Rose Reilly*, by Purple TV, written and directed by Margot McCuaig, was screened on BBC Alba.

On Friday 4th October 2019, in Reilly's hometown of Stewarton, an event was held celebrating her life. In front of family, friends and local people, pupils from local schools entertained Reilly with a musical show, honouring her many achievements. It was then announced that the sports centre, built around the pitch where she first displayed her skills as a three-year-old, was to be renamed the Rose Reilly Sports Centre. Reilly said, *"I gave away all my medals and trophies during my playing career, but having my local sports centre named after me … that's my legacy."*

On 4th November 2019, Ayrshire College presented Rose Reilly with an Honorary Fellowship Award for being an inspirational role model to young women in Ayrshire and beyond.

On 28th November 2019, at Glasgow Caledonian University, Reilly was made an Honorary Doctor of the University in recognition of her outstanding contribution to women's football.

In the New Year's Honours list 2020, Rose Reilly was awarded an MBE for services to women's football. However, delayed by COVID-19 pandemic restrictions, she was finally presented with the award on 19th January 2022, by HRH Princess Anne.[24]

On Monday 13th September 2021, the first performance of *Rose*, a play commissioned by A Play, A Pie and A Pint, took place at Òran Mór in Glasgow's West End. Written by Lorna Martin, directed by Maureen Carr, with the part of Rose played by Christina Strachan, the play was a huge success. On 28th April 2022 a sold-out performance raised the funds needed to take the play for a special performance in Italy. Produced by the English Theatre Milan on the Teatro Gerolamo in Piazza Beccaria, the production played to an enthusiastic audience.

In September 2022, Witsherface Productions toured the show throughout Scotland with Maureen Carr as Rose. For the majority of the performances of *Rose*, Reilly attended and took a Q&A session with the audience afterwards.

On Thursday 6th October 2022, the ladies of the first Scottish team to play England, known as the Ravenscraig Pioneers,

Rose, with Valentina and Norberto at the Palace of Holyroodhouse, Edinburgh, on her presentation of an MBE for services to women's football. 19th January 2022. Image with the permission of Rose Reilly.

celebrated the 50th anniversary of the match with a presentation at Hampden Park, the Scottish football national stadium. Prior to the FIFA Women's World Cup play-off against Austria, the ladies unveiled a mural celebrating the team of '72. After the unveiling, led by Elsie Cook, who has been the guiding light of women's football in Scotland and organiser of the first international game, the team joined the current Scottish players on the pitch for the playing of the national anthem.[25]

In December 2022, a pub named the *Rose Reilly* opened its doors on Albert Road, Govanhill, a popular route for football supporters to Hampden Park, Scotland's national stadium.

In 2023 BBC Scotland Sport broadcast *Icons of Scottish Football.*

Series 1:3, broadcast of 18th June, features Rose Reilly, "… *the only Scot to win the world cup".*

"I can't give advice, but don't listen to anybody, don't listen to your teachers, your tutors and anything like that. If you want to do something in life you do it, you do your best. It doesn't matter if you're a bank manager, doctor, nurse, the cleaner; if you do your best, it should be good enough for you. Don't try to impress anybody else, just impress yourself. Thank you."
Rose Reilly. November 2019.

References

1   In conversation with Rose Reilly. 4th January 2021, 27th June 2023.
2   Ibid.
3   *Nutmeg Magazine,* 17th July 2017. https://www.theguardian.com/football
4   Ibid.
5   *History of Women's Football,* Patrick Brennan. http://www.donmouth.co.uk/womens_football/1881.html
6   *Shekicks,* Women's football magazine. https://shekicks.net/40-years-ago-today-scotland-2-3-england/
7   *Nutmeg Magazine,* 17th July 2017. https://www.theguardian.com/football
8   *Daily Mirror,* 8th May 1975, p. 27. col. 1.
9   In conversation with Rose Reilly.
10 *Staffordshire Sentinel,* 31st January 1990, p.47 col.1–5.
11 *Sunday People,* 26th January 1975, p. 19. col. 1.
12 In conversation with Rose Reilly.
13 *Rose Reilly,* Purple TV, Dir Margot McCuaig. BBC Alba, 25th June 2019.
14 https://www.rsssf.com/tablesm/mundialito-women.html
15 https://www.rsssf.com/tablesw/wom-xian84.html
16 In conversation with Rose Reilly.
17 *Scotsman,* 12th November 2007. https://scotsman.com/sport/football/
18 *Liverpool Echo,* 7th January 1987, p. 19.
19 *Liverpool Echo,* 9th January 1987, p. 24. col. 3.
20 *Liverpool Echo,* 7th January 1987, p. 8. col. 1.
21 *The Herald, 12th May 2001.*
22 https://www.facebook.com/UniWestofScotland/
23 *The Herald,* 28th November 2019.
24 *Scotsman,* 2nd January 2020. https://scotsman.com/sport/football/
25 Scottish Football Association, Ravenscraig Pioneers.

Ben Parsonage with Albert.
© George Parsonage.

Ben and George Parsonage

BENJAMIN (Ben) Parsonage was born at 251 Nuneaton Street, Glasgow on the 16th February 1903. He was the first child of Benjamin Parsonage and his wife Annie Morrison, also from Glasgow. Benjamin worked manufacturing tube fittings.[1]

From a young age, Parsonage was a keen rower and an immensely powerful oarsman. At 5ft 1in, he wasn't tall, with his friends describing him as "*a pocket Hercules*", but what he lost in height he gained in strength. While still at school, he worked in a nearby mill, but he spent his spare time as a member of Clydesdale Rowing Club at the boatyard of the Glasgow Humane Society (GHS) in Glasgow Green by the River Clyde. By 1918 he was around the boatyard so often that he began unofficially assisting the officers of the GHS when emergency calls came in.[2]

When he left school, Parsonage began an apprenticeship as a boilermaker with Blythswood and Beardmore shipping companies, but the call of the river was too strong, driving him to spend all his free time at the boathouse.

His first rescue was in 1919. He was at the boats and saw somebody struggling in the water. Instinctively, he ran along the bank, dived in, and pulled the person out – a manner of rescue he must have seen George Geddes carry out numerous times. In this period, the Geddes family were the official officers of the GHA, the responsibility passing through the family line until 1928, with the tragic death of George Geddes Jnr, the last of the Geddes line.

As the river was in flood, George Geddes Snr told Parsonage there would be no hiring of boats or work done as the river flow was too strong, advising him instead to visit his mother on the other side of Glasgow Green, known to locals as 'the Green'. While he was away, George Geddes Jnr spotted a man in the water and, with the aid of a constable and a 15-year-old boy, rowed off to help the struggling man. After heavy rain, the water was wild and the current intense, making it exceptionally difficult to manoeuvre the boat. At one point they were thrown close enough to the casualty to allow the constable to grab the back of his coat collar, but the swirl of the water took the boat one way and the man the other, tearing him out of the constable's grasp. Without warning, George Geddes Jnr dived in, grabbing the victim as he hit the water, but the current took both away from the boat, dragging them under the surface. Seconds later, as the boat twisted in the vortex, the pair were briefly seen but were hauled down again almost immediately. It took several days of searching before Geddes's body was located. Old Mr Geddes, already very ill, watched the scene unfold and never recovered. Ben Parsonage became, in practical terms, the main officer from this time.

The Glasgow Humane Society is the oldest organisation of its kind in the world. Founded by Glasgow businessman James Coulter in 1760 with a donation of £200 to the Faculty of Surgeons (now the Royal College of Physicians and Surgeons of Glasgow), the organisation's aim was not only to rescue people from the river but to recover the bodies of those unfortunates who had drowned.[3]

In the second half of the 18th Century, parts of the river had a depth of only 38cm, at low water and 60cm, at high water, with as many as seven fords used for crossing from one bank to the other. However, strong winds regularly caused abnormally high water, making the river unpredictable and dangerous, especially to those on foot. One such extreme event occurred in 1882 when the river rose 6m above normal, flooding vast areas of the city and causing severe damage. Much of the land around Glasgow Cross and the

Green was peat bog and a danger to all who travelled and worked in the area.

Over the years, during construction work, several well-preserved canoes have been unearthed, far into the present-day city centre, confirming the belief by archaeologists that many areas of the city centre were under water in ancient times.

Some 230 years ago, not only was the River Clyde very different from the present-day river, but attitudes to those who were driven to take their own life were particularly harsh. In the eyes of the Church, those who committed suicide were doomed to hell and eternal damnation. Rarely did anyone go to the aid of someone struggling in the water for fear they would suffer the same fate. Those who entered the water, whether by a deliberate act or by accident, invariably drowned.

The early 18th century saw the influence of the Scottish Enlightenment among academics, and attitudes were changing. Francis Hutcheson, Professor of Moral Philosophy at Glasgow University in the 1730s, urged that, *"in all our work, the human condition should always be at the heart of our thinking"*. This created a wide movement away from church edicts.

As quoted by George Parsonage from the GHS records in his *Short History of the Glasgow Humane Society*,[4] *"That a Humane Society should have been established in 1790 in Glasgow is no doubt due to the influence of the medical faculty of the College. It may also be related to the Spirit of the age, the movement that developed throughout the eighteenth century and is known to us as 'the Enlightenment'"*.[5]

Many cities in Europe formed Humane Societies, distributing money to individuals who rescued or recovered victims from their waterways; however, it was only the GHS which employed an officer to *"carry out the practical work of prevention, rescue and recovery"*.

With the appointment of the first officer in 1790, the GHS was the only dedicated inland water rescue service in Britain and, most likely, Europe.

For the first 100 years of its existence, the work of the GHS was primarily carried out in the immediate area of Glasgow Green, as this was looked upon as the city centre. However, the development of the area around the Broomielaw, the continuing growth of the city as many merchants took their homes and business into Glasgow, and the increase in shipbuilding throughout the first half of the 1900s caused movement of the city centre towards the harbour. Dozens of paddle steamers attracted thousands of day-trippers every weekend and soon these steamers found themselves vying for space with cargo ships. As well as avoiding each other, steamers and cargo ships also had to make room for the many tugs and ferries scurrying around the water; it was a busy and chaotic place.[6]

With the vast numbers of people visiting or working in the area, many accidents happened; there were no guardrails, and it was all too easy on a crowded quayside to fall into the river. Historically, the harbour area was separated from the Green by a weir with no rescue boats kept below it. Those who found themselves in the water invariably became recoveries rather than rescues.

In the late 1800s, the GHS and several other vendors not only had rowing boats for hire but also springboards set into the banks where those seeking adventure could plunge into the river. It was due to the many drownings of the city's people as they swam and bathed that prompted calls from the GHS officers for the provision of places where young people could play safely in water. This compelled Glasgow Corporation to build the city's first swimming pool in in 1878, located in Greenhead Street, adjacent to the Green. Around this time, springboards were removed from the river. In 1939 work began on an Olympic-sized open-air swimming pool on

Glasgow Green, only to be cancelled on the outbreak of the Second World War.[7]

Parsonage was the only person who hired boats with the safety of his customers in mind. George Parsonage recalled, "*... other people would hire boats no matter what the current was like because that was their living, and the number of people that drowned in the 1800s must have been hundreds and hundreds*". Parsonage always liked to be on hand when his boats were out. In those days, children were generally not taught to swim, and a capsized boat would immediately be seen as an emergency situation. While the majority of boat hires stopped with the outbreak of the war, GHS allowed boat hires until the early 1970s, the last to provide the service.

As a competition rower, Parsonage was only permitted to row in two races before the ruling body decreed his position as an officer of GHS made him a professional. This decision disappointed him greatly, as he was recognised as a fast and powerful rower who would certainly have amassed an extensive collection of trophies.

Rowing was a very popular pastime, leading to many boats being on the river, which in turn meant accidents. Rowing club members were not exempt; in the 1930s and 1940s, club members were falling in "*by the dozen*". Parsonage didn't record them. As a rower, he didn't want the sport looked on as dangerous. He thought of rowing as intrinsically safe if rowers followed the safety advice of never leaving the boat. If it were to capsize the boat should be used as a flotation device. However, on occasion, old style fixings caused feet to be trapped, and a routine situation could quickly develop into a danger to life.

In the 1800s there were drownings in many clubs: George Parsonage recalls a letter received after the death of his father, "*... before Ben Parsonage came there were accidents, and a letter away back in 1932 ... a letter from the rowing club [City of Glasgow Rowing*

Ben Parsonage on the River Clyde. © George Parsonage.

Club] said since Ben Parsonage arrived on the river there have been no accidents." Throughout his time as an officer, Parsonage would organise and set rules for the good conduct of rowing clubs and others on the river, and be on hand to provide rescue services at times of regattas.

On 22nd December 1933, Benjamin Parsonage married Sarah Mulholland, from the Gallowgate area of the city, at the City of Glasgow Rowing Club, Glasgow Green. The couple had four children: Elizabeth, Benjamin, Ann and George.[8]

At this time, he was staying at 11 Templeton Street. This was a temporary arrangement as the Humane Society House on the Green was undergoing a major refurbishment; crucially, Templeton Street, situated on the edge of the Green, enabled a quick response in the event of emergency calls.

When the house was finally completed in 1936, it came with a medical room for treatment of rescues. Sarah took charge of each new patient. There were two beds, one with a rubber mattress and the other with blankets. Rescues were first put onto the bed with a rubber mattress, where Parsonage and Sarah would strip them of their wet clothes, dry them down and wrap them up in blankets while waiting for the ambulance to arrive. Ambulances could take some time, as they were not radio controlled. When the children were older, the whole family was involved in rescuing, reviving and comforting people.

The war years took their toll on everyone. The number of suicide attempts increased dramatically: men who had lived through the first world war and couldn't bear the thought of living through another, women trying to bring up children with little money and no man at home, women whose husbands never returned from the battlefield. Parsonage had to rescue or recover all of these unfortunates.

Accidental drownings also saw an increase during the harbour's shipbuilding peak. Wartime blackouts were particularly treacherous, and the docks became rife with accidents. Night watchmen and soldiers on guard duty, unfamiliar with the area, often fell victim.

During the war and post-war years, children became regular casualties. Many children, numbering in the hundreds, drowned in canals around the city. The majority of these fatalities occurred in the 1940s and early 1950s, prior to fathers returning home. Mothers and grandmothers were left to support families, resulting in many children playing unsupervised, often with the temptation of a nearby canal. Most canals around Glasgow were filled during the 1960s and 1970s, leaving little of the canal system remaining, a system which has in modern times become popular and well used again. In George Parsonage's words, *"A busy canal is also a safe canal, as there's always somebody about. And you've also got to remember that children nowadays don't really go out to play."* There are now very few child fatalities.

One of the biggest innovations in the job of a GHS Officer wasn't modern technology in the form of GPS or radios; it came in the form of a simple towbar. Previously, a lorry had to be hired to carry the boat, wasting precious time before travelling any distance. During the 1930s and 1940s, rescues weren't carried out in the harbour area or other parts of the city, and the delay in getting to the scene meant the recovery of a body. However, in the 1950s, police produced towbars for cars; this simple piece of equipment, attached to the back of a police vehicle, transformed the way Parsonage worked. No longer restricted to the area of Glasgow Green, speedy travel meant it was possible that rescues could be carried out farther afield.

George Parsonage summed up the situation, *"In the 1950s, Father became quite incredible. Between early 1950 and when he died in 1979, how that man ever carried out the work he did, I will never know. He really was racing around, putting his clothes on in the back of a police car and some of the things he did to get to the person in the water ... but we've never seen anybody drown, we've always been on time. If somebody was alive when we arrived, we got them out. I became a bit eccentric trying to keep that."*

Parsonage assisted and advised police on recovery of items thrown into the river many times, but in the search for weapons used by mass murderer Peter Manuel magnets were used by Parsonage for the first time. Two days were spent on a barge, searching with a powerful electromagnet, enabled by an electrical supply brought to the water's edge. They found two handguns, but not the type sought by the police. Finally, at Parsonage's suggestion, a diver was a brought in. After a briefing by Parsonage that the gun was likely to be stuck between boulders on the river bed, a gun was quickly found. It played a vital role in Manuel's conviction. Many weapons were subsequently found by Parsonage or his son George, and magnets are now used on a regular basis, usually in the search for murder weapons, and often successfully. A set of car keys much sought after by the police were located, as was a stolen car radio.[9] [10]

A wide variety of items have been taken from the water by Parsonage: a human skull, parts of a human skeleton, newborn babies, dismembered bodies in sacks, dead cows, horses, dogs, donkeys. Once, in 1963, a pup became trapped on one of the piers at the Albert Bridge and was rescued by Parsonage. He waited the statutory 30 days, and when the dog wasn't claimed, he was named Albert and stayed with the family for the following 12 years.[11]

On Monday 1st October 1979, Ben Parsonage BEM, died suddenly, aged 79, in his house on Glasgow Green, overlooking his beloved River Clyde.

Officially, he had worked as an officer of the Glasgow Humane Society for 51 years, rarely leaving his base at the house on Glasgow Green. With the addition of his 10 unofficial years, for over 60 years Ben Parsonage lived and breathed the GHS philosophy of Prevention, Rescue and Recovery. He recovered in the region of 1,000 bodies from the waters in and around Glasgow and rescued at least 1,500 people from drowning.

His funeral, on Thursday 4th October, was attended by representatives from all walks of life. The cortege to St Andrews Church was led by a police car flanked by mounted officers. Hundreds of Glaswegians stood silently in the pouring rain as the congregation packed into the church where Ben Parsonage's eldest daughter Elizabeth played the organ. After the service, the cortege travelled slowly through Glasgow Green and the GHA boathouse where rowers saluted the hearse as it passed, continuing on a road lined by officers to Rutherglen Cemetery, where Ben Parsonage was laid to rest overlooking the River Clyde.

George Parsonage was born in the Glasgow Humane Society House on 15th October 1943. His earliest memories are of sitting at an upstairs window watching his father at work on the boats. It was impossible not to become involved in a rescue, recalling memories of being barely old enough to carry the stretcher he'd been sent to fetch. Along with his older sisters, Elizabeth and Ann, he'd been taught to row from a very early age and assisted his father in rescues by the time he reached his teens.

Like his father before him, George Parsonage was a powerfully fast rower and sculler. A member of the Clydesdale Amateur Rowing Club, he won approximately 800 races and 130 championships in his career, dominating Scottish sculling for approximately 10 years from 1968. He was also a major influence on British sculling.[12]

(In rowing, a rower handles a single oar, a sculler uses two oars.)

As Scottish sculling champion, he won the Head of River race on the River Tyne, from Clara Vale to Stella in 1967 and 1968,and was awarded the Ture Hillerstrom Cup. He continues to hold the record for the Clyde Head of the River Race set in 1967. He was part of the crew that set the fastest time sculling across the Irish Sea, a distance of 89 miles, completed in 14 hours 7 minutes.[13]

Amongst his proudest achievements, he set Guinness World Records in 1975 for a single-scull of Loch Ness, a distance of 23 miles in a time of 2 hours 43 minutes. This was a sponsored event to raise money for both a multiple sclerosis charity, and funds for Whitehill Secondary School. In 1993, 18 years after breaking the record George, rowing double-scull with Peter Haining, set a new record of 2 hours 28 minutes.[14] [15]

As a child, George dismantled his toys to see how they worked, and as he grew older, he used the workshop at his father's boathouse to transform pieces of scrap and discarded metal recovered from the river into extraordinary works of art. His work was termed junk sculpture and earned George a coveted position on the sculpture course at Glasgow School of Art.

He'd already been offered a place on the architecture course at Strathclyde University and found a position in an architect's office, but when the offer from the School of Art came along, he immediately accepted. George completed his course in 1967, being awarded both the Henderson Scholarship and the John Keppie Travelling Scholarship, which allowed him to spend several months studying in Europe, mainly in Italy.

Completing a teaching degree at Jordanhill College allowed George to teach art at Whitehill School in Glasgow, a career that spanned almost 26 years.

If he had any reservations about following in his father's footsteps, they were dispelled when an emergency call came in on the afternoon of his father's death. Without hesitation, George ran to the boats and headed off to help with the rescue; it was a responsibility and a duty, not only to his father but to his mother and sister, Ann. He had assumed his father's role.

It was often suggested that Ben Parsonage had a sixth sense that alerted him to trouble in the water. When asked if his father's intuition may have been passed on to him, George replied, "*It's quite uncanny. You get a feeling. You say, I'm going over to the shops to get a paper, then you say no, and sit down, and just as you sit down, the bell goes to tell you somebody's in the water. Or you decide to go somewhere, but there's just something, something totally completely uncanny. I've seen it happen with my dad so often, and yes, it does happen to me. Things happen for the strangest reasons. Yes.*"

George continued, "*An example of it was when I rescued a woman*

123

and her child. I said to my dad, 'I'm taking my slim boat and I'm only going up' – we always said where we were going, what we were doing; he knew where we were all the time – 'I'm only going up to Rutherglen Bridge' ... and turning at Rutherglen Bridge, when about seven or eight hundred yards up river I saw splashing in the water and ... I reckon that's the fastest ... that's the day I decided that ... it's a bit cliched to talk like this but I decided that day that I had been made a very, very fast sculler not to win races but to do rescues. I started sprinting, got up there, dived off the boat into the water, got hold of the woman who fought back like mad and I realised her four-year-old son had sunk so I really had to shove her, really shove her away, get rid of her. I did a surface dive, and I went down about 20ft ... a long surface dive ... and amazingly found the boy, came back up to the surface and started giving him mouth-to-mouth resuscitation.

"*I had him on one side and grabbed her with my other hand and started swimming back with both of them, and then, at that moment, my dad arrived. A few seconds later, he said, 'I wondered where you were and I knew something was wrong.' Uncanny, he knew exactly what happened. The janitor from the school ran down; he'd seen what was happening from his window and ran down to help us out the water.*"

Together, they successfully managed to resuscitate the child. The mother had seen her son fall into the water, and instinctively jumped in to save him, but couldn't get to him before he disappeared beneath the surface. Fortunately for all concerned, George was on hand. Using every piece of his knowledge of the water, his skill and strength, but most of all, his selfless, instinctive bravery, made this one of the most joyful of his many rescues.

George met his wife Stephanie, then an international rower, when she capsized while training on the River Clyde. They have two sons, Benjamin and Christopher. After their marriage, there was never a need to use the medical room in the house for those rescued. Thanks to the advances in communication from the 1980s, an ambulance always arrived at the scene of an incident with fully trained personnel and the most modern equipment by the time a person had been rescued. *"In Stephanie's time, the ambulance has always been there. That's a wonderful record for the ambulance, absolutely marvellous."*

Technology, initially in the form of a pager, and later a mobile phone, allowed George a freedom his father never enjoyed. Ben Parsonage had been tied to the vicinity of the boathouse at Glasgow Green for all his working life, rarely permitting himself the luxury of a trip to the cinema, family meal or celebration, or even a honeymoon.

George gratefully accepted an arrangement offered by the Director of Education, allowing him to be on call and available for GHS work throughout his teaching career. This concession worked very well; he parked his car adjacent to the art classes, enabling him to be on his way without delay when called. When work for the GHS and teaching responsibilities clashed, the Education Department suggested working a four-day week, but George felt that was unfair to other teachers and accepted an offer of early retirement in 1993. This settlement allowed a continuation of a way of life he had grown up with; he could work on his sculpture and art while being available at a moment's notice for the GHS.

In 1993 George Parsonage, with George McCracken, founded the Glasgow Water Safety Working Group, joined by individuals and organisations with a personal or business interest in the waterways around Glasgow. The group's aim was to make contact directly with companies based along the riverside and encourage them to keep safety equipment on their premises. Today, the group raises and liaises on issues with Glasgow City Council.[16]

In 1999 George Parsonage was invited to the inaugural meeting of the River Clyde Working Group and given the position of advisor.

An ongoing goal for the group had been to encourage rowers who use the river to act in a safe manner. The GHS, with Glasgow City Council, the Water Safety Group, and the agreement and endorsement of the rowing clubs who use the river, developed *Rules and Guidelines for Safe Use of the River Clyde by Rowing Clubs*, which was agreed in 1999. All clubs who wish to row on this area of water are now obliged to comply with the regulations.

In 2005 a meeting was held with representatives of Police Scotland and Scottish Fire and Rescue, declaring that as the GHS Officer was working alone, health and safety guidance meant that the agencies could no longer utilise the GHS Officer for rescue and recovery. In 2007 the River Clyde Water Rescue Centre, operated by Scottish Fire and Rescue Service, opened a new base at the Glasgow College of Nautical Studies. George is pragmatic about the changes, noting the large amounts of funding provided to create the changes in the service: "*Having four rescue boats located at various points downstream of the weir and dozens of personnel trained in water rescue has to be a good thing.*"[17]

George Parsonage's assistant, William Graham, was promoted to full-time GHS Officer in 2015 and continues to liaise and assist the Scottish Fire and Rescue Service and Police Scotland when required. He continues the core work of prevention and safety on the water for a number of events, such as regattas, races and commercial events taking place in the city, such as TRNSMT Festival.

For many years, the GHS has lobbied for some form of continuing benefit to the city of Glasgow after major exhibitions, conferences and iconic events, such as the Glasgow Garden Festival (1988), the Commonwealth Games (2014) and the UN Climate Change Conference COP26 (2021). It is hoped that the legacy from the COP26 Conference could be the continuing use of the additional security cameras which were installed covering both banks of the river.

George retired as an officer in 2019 and currently serves as a safety consultant on the rivers and waterways around the city, and has initiated several schemes over the past years.

George recalls the sad story of a couple and their daughter who were going home via the Glasgow Bridge after a nice day out and meal in the city. On the bridge, the father decided he could walk along the top rail of the balustrade, perhaps showing off a little to his daughter. It took only a slight gust of wind to knock him off balance and fall to his death in front of his horrified wife and child. It's likely if the top rail of the balustrade hadn't been so wide or flat, but perhaps rounded, or angled, there would have been no temptation for this father to expose himself to such danger.

Sadly, he is by no means the only person who has fallen into the water by walking along, sitting or climbing on a riverside fence. Despite many years of lobbying, George maintains that there are many faults in the design of protective features along the River Clyde and he continues to urge architects and planners to make it difficult for anyone to access a dangerous position. To this end, a booklet, *Architectural Handbook for Safe Waterways*,[18] has been produced by the GHS to aid designers and it's hoped that legislation will ensure all developers must incorporate the advice contained into planning applications.

The booklet encourages planners and architects to consider the prime aim of the GHS, as highlighted in the introduction. *"Design should allow every citizen and visitor the right to be able to walk our waterway paths in the knowledge that every reasonable precaution against them inadvertently falling into the river has been taken and that adequate public rescue equipment is in position and readily available should they require to use it."*

George Parsonage © Glasgow Humane Society.

As an officer of the GHS, the siting and use of lifebelts and safety equipment has been at the forefront of George's experience.[19] In 2005 a distressed woman called the emergency services several times from the River Kelvin Walkway but was unable to give her location. She was found murdered some time after her repeated 999 calls. George subsequently worked with Police Scotland and Glasgow City Council to devise a simple system where every lifebelt and safety ladder position clearly displays a designated number which, when given to a 999 operator, will immediately show on their screen not only the precise location, but nearest access roads, hospitals, etc. This system can be rolled out throughout the country.[20]

Between George Parsonage and his father, they rescued in the region of 3,000 people from the waters of Glasgow and have both been awarded multiple bravery awards. George explains there may well have been some duplication of the numbers when they worked together: "*I didn't realise there were so many until I was at the Royal Humane Society in London to receive a lifetime achievement medal; even at that I do not know the amount rescued, especially in my father's time, primarily because he was kept too busy to write it all down.*"[21]

Fame of their work has spread worldwide, with Australian folk singer duo Mundy-Turner writing and dedicating the song 'The Riverman' to George after viewing a television documentary on his life. Parsonage Square and Parsonage Row can be found in Glasgow's Merchant City area.[22]

George Geddes Parsonage, MBE, DipA, DUniv, MUniv is a founder member of the Swimming Teachers' Association (STA) and a certified member of the International Federation of Swimming Teachers Associations (IFSTA). Despite a debilitating illness diagnosed in 2019, George continues to work tirelessly in promoting, educating, and campaigning for the safety of all those who live, work, and play on or around the River Clyde.

12 REMARKABLE SCOTS

Ben Parsonage

1930. Anchor Line Bravery Award.

1936. Glasgow Corporation Bravery Medal.

1939–1945. Defence Medal.

1953. Glasgow Corporation Bravery Medal Bar.

1955. Glasgow Corporation Bravery Medal Second Bar.

1971. British Empire Medal. BEM.

George Parsonage

1971. Glasgow Corporation Bravery Medal.

1972. Royal Humane Society. Honorary Testimonial of the Society for Bravery.

1978. Strathclyde Region Bravery Medal and Bar.

1982. Royal Lifesaving Society Commonwealth Council. Mountbatten Medal.

1983. Royal Humane Society. Honorary Testimonial of the Society for Bravery.

1995. Foyle Search and Rescue. For Dedication to the Preservation of Life.

1997. St Mungo Medal.

1998. Strathclyde Police 'A' Division. Working with officers for the Protection of Life.

1999. Member of the British Empire Medal. MBE.

2002. Queens Golden Jubilee Medal.

2002. Coastguard Medal.

2004. Royal Humane Society. Honorary Testimonial of the Society for Bravery.

2005. Royal Humane Society. Lifetime Achievement Silver Award.

2006. Royal Lifesaving Society Commonwealth Council. Service Cross.

2006. University of Strathclyde. Honorary Doctor of the University.

2006. Glasgow Caledonian University. Honorary Master of the University.

2012. Queen Diamond Jubilee Medal.

2020. Daily Record Pride of Scotland Special Recognition Award.

References

1 Conversations with George Parsonage. 18th & 27th October, 17th December 2021, 10th August 22.

2 Parsonage, George; *Rescue His Business The Clyde His Life: The Story of Ben Parsonage.* (Glasgow, 1990)

3 https://www.glasgowhumanesociety.org.uk

4 https://www.parsonageriverman.com/histories

5 Herman, Arthur, *The Scottish Enlightenment.* (London, 2003)

6 Shields, John; *Clyde Built.* (Glasgow, 1949)

7 *Glasgow Herald*, 20th February 1874, p. 4. col. 6.

8 *Tales of the Riverman 45.* George Parsonage.

9 *Birmingham Gazette*, 20th January 1958, p. 29. col. 5.

10 *Aberdeen Evening Express*, 30th April 1962, p. 5. col. 6.

11 Parsonage, George, *Rescue His Business*. p. 170.

12 *Aberdeen Evening Express*, 13th June 1975, p. 20. co. 5.

13 *Newcastle Journal*, 4th November 1968, p. 10. col. 5.

14 *Aberdeen Press and Journal*, 14th April 1993, p. 2 col. 8

15 *Aberdeen Evening Express*, 17th May 1975, p.1 col 4

16 https://www.parsonageriverman.com/histories

17 Ibid

18 https://www.parsonageriverman.com/resources

19 https://www.parsonageriverman.com/images/Resources/gps.pdf

20 *BBC News*, 6th February 2006.

21 *Holyrood Magazine*, 2nd December 2019. Article.

22 *Trades House Newsletter*. Riverman Concert, p. 2.

Mary Slessor, from Mary Slessor of Calabar
Published by Hodder and Stoughton Ltd, 1923.

Mary Slessor

MARY Mitchell Slessor was born on 2nd December 1848 in her grandmother's house in Mutton Brae, Gilcomston, Aberdeen, the second of seven children to Robert Slessor, a shoemaker of Buchan, and his wife Mary Mitchell, a weaver of Old Meldrum.

Robert was an alcoholic, and in 1859, after losing his job in Buchan, he moved the family to Dundee to look for work, finding accommodation at 17 Harriet Street in a desperately poor and run-down area of the city.[1]

Robert briefly found work in one of the city's many textile mills, but his drinking problem took hold and he lost this job. Slessor and her older brother Robert soon found work at the Baxter Brothers' Lower Dens Mill.[2]

The Scotland Education Act of 1872 called on employers to provide educational facilities for the children in their employment. Slessor was initially known as a halftimer, working half the day and attending school the other half. When she was older and working full time, six in the morning to six in the evening, she followed her shift in the factory with several more hours in the classroom. Slessor loved to learn; she avidly read all the books she could lay her hands on, often propping a book on her loom to read when she could find time. By the age of 14, she was an experienced, and relatively well-paid weaver and became the family's main breadwinner.[3]

Slessor's mother was a devout Presbyterian who, along with the children, attended the local United Free Presbyterian Church where the family would look forward to reading each new issue of their *Missionary Magazine*. Here, she read of the exploits of David Livingstone, who had become a national hero. Inspired, Slessor applied to the Foreign Mission Board for a position in Africa, but the life of a missionary was seen as men's work, forcing her to become a volunteer teacher at Quarry Pend Mission in the city. [4]

Slessor's older brother was accepted to become a missionary, but died before he could take up his place. This, along with the death of Livingstone in 1873, and the resultant publicity of his funeral in Westminster Abbey, only made her more determined than ever to follow what she saw as her life's calling. Displaying the iron will that characterised her throughout her years in Africa, she continued to put pressure on the Foreign Mission Board for an overseas posting until, in 1875, they granted her a missionary posting as a teacher at the Calabar Mission in Duke Town, Calabar, Nigeria. After three months' training at Moray House, Edinburgh, on 5th August 1876, she sailed for West Africa on board the SS *Ethiopia*.

This posting provided an enormous cultural challenge for Slessor; she worked among the local women and, discovering an aptitude for the language, soon conversed with them in their own Efik dialect. Taking the time and trouble to learn the language and being able to converse fluently was a major factor in her blossoming relationship with the native people.

Slessor held the view that to understand the people, she had to live as they did and, determined to be like the natives, she drank unboiled water, walked barefoot, and refused to use a mosquito net or even wear a hat.[5]

Being as close to the native people as possible, and in particular the women, she felt best able to understand the customs and culture of the local tribes. She soon realised that the tribes had their own codes of conduct and ideas of justice that were far removed from those she regarded as civilised. Slessor found that she had to "*... teach the first principles of everything*". Before long, she also understood the extreme brutality of the hold witchcraft had on the people.

Normally, workers in the mission fields enjoyed a return home every four years, but suffering from frequent bouts of fever, and homesickness, she returned to Scotland in June 1879. In her time at home, Slessor took the opportunity to settle her mother and sister to Downfield, a village close to Dundee. She was still the primary source of income for the family, with half her salary contributing to the upkeep of their home.

Recovered and happy that her family was settled, after an absence of sixteen months Slessor returned to Calabar in October 1880. She found that her persistent petitioning of the Foreign Missionary Committee had been successful with news that they had put her in charge of the mission at Old Town. This was a huge step up for her; the opportunity to run the mission with her own ideas and methods. The scale of the challenge became apparent when, on her return to the town, she was greeted with the sight of a human skull on a pole at the entrance.

One belief held by the tribespeople appalled Slessor – the custom of twin-murder. Locals believed that the birth of twins resulted from a coupling with evil spirits, and as such, both mother and babies were cursed. The natives believed that one of the babies belonged to the devil; keeping the tribe safe meant breaking the child's back and crushing its body into a calabash, or water-pot, before throwing the remains into the bush to be devoured by wild beasts and insects. The murdered child couldn't leave through the doorway, as that would put a curse on anyone coming into or leaving the hut, but through a hole made in the back wall, sealed afterwards. Often a twin-baby was simply left in an open space in the bush to be eaten alive. If they couldn't decide which child carried the evil spirits, both were murdered and the mother cast out of tribal society, fated to live alone in the bush, unable to use any pathways for fear the paths would become cursed and unusable. [6]

Slessor spent much of her life teaching, cajoling, and preaching against this abhorrent practice, becoming a rescuer of these unfortunate babies and a carer for the abandoned women. She adopted some of these children despite advice to the contrary from mission societies. As was usual for her, she followed her heart and trusted her own instincts. It is estimated that by 1890 she had saved around 50 sets of twins.

Towards the end of 1882, a ferocious tornado hit Old Town, damaging Slessor's house to the extent that she could no longer live there, forcing her to find refuge in a factory. The Presbytery insisted on her return to Duke Town, only to discover when she arrived that her illness gave them no alternative but to send her home for treatment and rest. She left for Scotland in April 1883, so frail that she had to be carried on board, and so weak there were fears she wouldn't survive the journey.[7]

Slessor insisted on bringing with her the first twin-girl she had rescued, fearing for her safety in her absence. Slessor had originally rescued both twins, a boy and a girl, but once, when she had to leave the house for a short time, the girl's twin brother was taken and killed. Slessor named the girl Janie, after her sister of the same name. When she was older, she became known as Jean.

A lecture tour was arranged around the country in 1884 to bring notice of Slessor's work to the general public. The girl accompanied Slessor, resulting in a chattering Jean, who spoke her English with a Dundee accent, becoming the main attraction. So much money was being donated on the tour that the Foreign Missions Board asked Slessor to postpone her return to Calabar, but she declined, desperate to return to her people in Nigeria.

Just as she was making plans to return to Creek Town, Slessor discovered that her youngest sister Janie, was very ill with tuberculosis. On the suggestion that the harsh climate in Dundee was holding back her sister's recuperation and, as the south of England presented a much milder climate, Slessor rented a house in Topsham in Devon. There, Slessor arranged care for both her mother and sister with the help of the local Congregational Church and a Christian lady in the area. The three were hardly settled in the house when news came of the sudden death of her sister Susan in Edinburgh, leaving Slessor as the sole breadwinner for the family.

With this in mind, she decided the time was right to return to Creek Town. Slessor and Jean returned to Calabar in November 1885; she had been back for only a month when her mother died unexpectedly, followed weeks later by the death of Janie, her last remaining sibling. Within three months, Slessor had lost all remaining members of her family.[8]

In August 1888, she decided to move north, up-country to Okoyong. This area of the continent was still very much regarded as dangerous territory, described as "... *a noisome land of obnoxious forest and savage tribes who are given over to cruel superstition, debased fetichism, and evil custom"*. Many missionaries before her had perished at the hands of native tribesmen, fierce people known to be head-hunters who ate the flesh of their conquests. Slessor relished the challenge. Her pioneering spirit believed that a woman could succeed where so many men before her had failed; she believed a woman would be accepted more readily by the tribes than a man, and seen as posing less of a threat to the local chiefs.[9]

Now responsible for several outstations, every Sunday Slessor would trek through the jungle to conduct a service at each village, her native assistants leading the way, beating drums for all to hear, announcing Slessor's arrival.[10]

To a casual observer she may have looked small and weak, but this red-haired Scot had a fearlessness, combined with an iron will, that made even the most savage of men stop and listen. She would walk out onto the battlefield, excited natives all around her, holding up her arms, signalling in no uncertain terms to stop. A story said to be typical of the woman tells of her intervention in a dispute between two tribes that was about to escalate into violence.[11]

"*'Come here, you!' she said to a man who, with his gun up, was about to fire. 'Give me that gun, and go and find your chief and bring him here!' Then, telling her followers to clear the long grass away and put up her chair, she marched across to where the enemy was lined up behind the mud walls of the village, and, calling for the chief, she insisted that he come immediately, as she wished to speak to him.*

"Reluctantly the chief appeared. Taking hold of his arm, she marched him back to her chair which was placed under a shady tree in a clearing. She motioned to the chief whom she had brought along from the village to sit down on her left, when from the bushes on the right appeared the other chief followed by a crowd of his armed men, wildly gesticulating. Mary Slessor had sat down in the meantime, but she got up again and told the newly arrived leader of the warriors to send his men back into the woods. She wanted him alone. Was he afraid of her that he brought so many men? Reluctantly the tribesmen withdrew, scowling and growling, the newly arrived leader sat down on a mat at her right."

Slessor's tactic on these occasions was to sit, often knitting, while the chiefs talked. "*They loved to talk,*" she would say. "*They could talk all night.*" And once the 'palaver' was done with, 'Ma Slessor' called a verdict and the chiefs would agree. The chiefs sealed the agreement with a blood-letting ceremony; a warrior from each tribe drained blood from their hand, mixed it with the other, and served half each to their chiefs to drink. This blood covenant sealed the peace between both tribes.

Slessor commented, "*It seems sometimes to be miraculous that hordes of armed, drunken, passion-swayed men, should give heed and chivalrous honour to a woman.*"

In 1889 the British Government formed the Niger Coast Protectorate and announced that a vice-consul would take control of the area. Slessor complained, arguing that her people were not ready to obey British law. Surprisingly, the consul agreed, appointing Slessor herself as Vice-Consul of Okoyong, which gave her the power to preside over the native court. Later, in 1905, she became the

A Section of the Mary Slessor Memorial Window.
With permission of the McManus, Dundee's Art Gallery and Museum.
Photograph by Jerry Brannigan.

vice-president of the Ikot Obong Native Court. This appointment made Mary Slessor the first female magistrate in the British Empire.[12]

With her fluency in the language, the role suited Slessor very well and enabled her to solve many disputes, protect women who had few rights, and become involved in the making of both local and national government policy. She successfully encouraged tribes to trade with one another, and it has been reported that she was instrumental in encouraging the start of oil export from Nigeria. She said it was much better to export oil than import countless cases of gin to the detriment of the people.

Slessor had worked with the tribes in her area trying, with some success, to put a stop to trial by ordeal as a method to determine the guilt or otherwise of their men and women. A native, often a woman, had boiling oil poured over their arm, with a guilty verdict delivered if they showed any pain. Slessor suggested to the chiefs that even they, great men as they were, might show pain if she were to get boiling oil and pour it over their arms.

Slessor won the complete trust of the native people; they came from long distances to bring their troubles to her, and unfailingly she straightened out the problem. When there were difficulties which the natives could not solve, they invariably turned to their 'White Mother'.[13]

In 1891, on a visit to England, Slessor shocked her friends by announcing that she was engaged to Mr Charles W Morrison of the Duke Town Mission. The couple had become engaged before she left Okoyong and hoped, on her return, they could work there together. The Mission Board asked Slessor if she would work in Duke Town with Morrison, who trained mission staff and whose work was looked upon as important. Slessor's reply was an unqualified no.

"I could not leave my work for such a reason. … If God does not send him up here then he must do his work and I must do mine where we have been placed."

A matter of a few months later, Morrison had to return to Scotland on health grounds. Unable to return to Africa. Morrison moved to North Carolina where a fire in a cabin he was living in destroyed all his literary papers. Morrison died shortly after.[14]

An overwhelming workload, combined with failing health, forced her decision in November 1909 to resign from the role as vice-president of the Itu Native Court. Slessor continued to petition Charles Partridge, the district commissioner of Calabar, about injustices and disputes, more especially those concerning the rights of women whom she continually campaigned for. Partridge said of her, *"She can go where no white man dare go. She can sway people when we cannot sway them."*

Slessor worked tirelessly against the cruelty of the tribal belief in witchcraft. In raids on other tribes, they often took slaves, slaves whose lives were looked upon as worthless. When a chief died, custom demanded that relatives would accompany him to the spirit land, meaning that his wives and slaves were buried with him. At the burial of one chief, there were the dead bodies of six female slaves below and six above his body. Slessor curtailed this custom by explaining to chiefs that they did not need slaves to lead them to their God when they died, resulting in a complaint by one elderly chief that *"… before you came, a man took his people with him, now he must go alone"*.

She frequently put her life at risk by interfering with a ceremony, pleading for the lives of women and children doomed to be used as a human sacrifice in a ritual or burial. It is reported that on one occasion, *"After an outburst of fighting at Ekenge a number of women were herded into a stockade, and men were proceeding to murder them. Mary Slessor heard of it and hurried to the scene. She got inside the stockade and held the armed men at bay. All day and night she stood in a tornado of rain. … Her courage broke the stubbornness of the men"*.

When traveller and writer Mary Kingsley visited her at Ekenge in 1895, she commented on her sunburnt face and dishevelled appearance, writing that *"Miss Slessor, … bullies the native chiefs in their own tongue, and is regarded by the other missionaries as mad and dangerous"*. However, Mary Kingsley continued, *"Ma Okoyong, I admire you, the greatest and most Christian woman of this coast. I would give anything to have your faith, … she was called Ma Okoyong, meaning Mother of all, by multitudes. She was a woman of great common-sense and fearlessness"*.[15]

When Slessor returned to Britain in 1891, she went first to Topsham to visit the graves of her mother and sister. Jean accompanied her, now old enough to act as her companion and carer. Slessor surprised many with her announcement that she had become engaged to Charles Morrison, fellow missionary at Duke Town, and 18 years her junior. However, when the missionary board refused to allow him to join her at Okoyong, the relationship collapsed, as Slessor could never leave her children and the rescued women.

Recovery from an attack of influenza and bronchitis delayed their return, but looked after by the Congregational Church in Devon, her health soon improved, allowing Slessor and Jean's journey to Calabar in February 1892.

By 1896 Slessor had decided to move her mission to Akap, six miles from the nearest landing site at Ikunetu by the Cross River. A market had opened in the town, and taking advantage of the movement of the local population, Slessor decided she had to be where the people lived, and began construction of a new mission house. However, sickness had spread amongst the children, quickly worsening when an epidemic of smallpox swept through the country.[16]

For hours every day, Slessor vaccinated as many of her people as possible, but the effects of the epidemic were relentless. As hundreds of the people in the country succumbed to the virus, all those affected went to Ma Okoyong for help, while those who were able made their escape from the country. A few days later, the men came to build the mission house to find a deathly silent village and an utterly exhausted Slessor. There was not a soul to be seen and many corpses to be buried.

To aid her recovery, the Mission Committee decided to send Slessor home while the mission was being rebuilt. Reluctant to leave the children, she took four with her: Mary, Alice, Maggie and Janie, and set off for Liverpool in early 1898, returning in December of the same year.

In her early 60s, Slessor was struck by rheumatoid arthritis, which curtailed many of her strenuous activities and forced her into an extended period of rest. Despite being urged to return to Scotland by her friends and fellow missionaries, or even to move to the relative comfort of Duke Town, Slessor, now with no family or emotional ties to Scotland, refused to leave her mission.

At the beginning of January 1915, Slessor became very unwell with a recurrence of fever. One of her girls went to seek help and a messenger was sent to Itu, summoning Dr Robertson. Over the following days the doctor attended Slessor but there was no cure; illness and fever had taken its toll on her exhausted body. Her final hours were reported, *"As the evening wore on, she became quieter, but had a great thirst, and begged that a little bit of the ice might be put into her mouth. … There was no great struggle at the end; just a gradual diminishing of the forces of nature, and Ma Akamba, 'The Great Mother,' entered into the presence of the King."*

On the 13th January 1915, Mary Mitchell Slessor died of fever and dysentery in her mud hut in the village of Use Ikot Oku, at 3.30am, surrounded and nursed by the mothers and girls she had saved. Janie, a baby deemed worthless in the eyes of her tribe, grew up to be Slessor's friend and assistant; a companion who carried her through the jungle, cared for her when she became ill, and sat beside her as she died.

By daylight, hearing the mournful cries of Slessor's girls, all the people of the village came to the house to share their grief, and as the news spread many people came from Itu and the surrounding district to see in death, *"… her who had been Eka kpukpru owo, 'Everybody's Mother'."*[17]

By morning, the news had been received by her friend Rev Wilkie at Duke Town and a launch was dispatched. While it was on the way, an English and an Efik service was being held at Itu. The launch arrived at 5.30pm, the coffin was placed on board, and the return voyage began.

Slessor's body reached Duke Town at midnight and lay at Government Beach until dawn. She was given a state funeral with Government officials, merchants, and missionaries all in attendance. The boys of the Training Institute were drawn up on the beach, policemen were posted in the streets, and the pupils of Duke Town school continued the line to the cemetery. All flags flew at half-mast, and the town lay hushed and still. The coffin, draped with the Union Flag, was carried shoulder high by the boat boys, wearing black singlets and

The Mary Slessor Commemorative Standing Stone.
In the grounds of The Steeple Church, Dundee.
© Jerry Brannigan.

mourning loin-cloths but no caps. Great crowds watched the procession, which moved along in silence.[18]

Mary Slessor was laid to rest beside the graves of two Scottish missionaries in Eyamba Street Cemetery, where a large stone cross dominates the surrounding area.

Inscribed on her headstone:

In loving memory of Mary Mitchell Slessor
Born Aberdeen 2 December 1848
Died at Use, Calabar 13 January 1915
For 38 years a heroic and devoted missionary chiefly among the
up-river tribes of this land. The people that walked in darkness
have seen a great light. They that turn many to righteousness
shall shine as the stars of the sun for ever and ever.

In 1913 King George V awarded Mary Slessor the Order of St John of Jerusalem, a Royal Order of Chivalry first constituted by Royal Charter from Queen Victoria in 1888. Humanitarian in its aims, it is an order motivated by Christian ideals.[19]

On 16th February 1916, Dundee Town Council unanimously approved a proposal to install a commemorative tablet at No. 6 Queen Street, the building where she engaged in her first mission.[20]

The McManus Galleries, Dundee's Art Gallery and Museum, displays the Mary Slessor Memorial Window, a stained-glass window that depicts events from her life. Unveiled on 28th September 1923, crowds flocked to the Victoria Art Galleries, as the Museum was then named. Although a gathering of around 450 was expected, long before the appointed hour the corridors and rooms of the building were crammed with men and women who wanted to pay their respects to Mary Slessor's memory.[21] [22]

In the early hours of the 10th August 1939, the window was vandalised and damaged when stones were thrown through it. A few hours later, John Fife (29), appeared at a police court charged with malicious damage, with the Fiscal asking that Fife be detained for medical observation. The original designer of the window, Mr William Aikman, who had learned of the damage in newspaper columns, offered to carry out the repairs himself.[23] [24]

On the 6th June 1953, shortly after the coronation of Queen Elizabeth II, the Coronation Bible Exhibition was held in the Chapter House of Westminster Abbey. Among the many historic and iconic copies of the bible on display was one belonging to Mary Slessor. She owned several bibles, and this copy was, as were the others, annotated throughout with notes in Efik and English in the margins. One of her bibles, thought to date from 1910, is on display at the McManus Museum in Dundee.

In September 1953, the Mary Slessor Corner opened as a permanent display at Dundee Museum (now the McManus). It contains a recording of Slessor's voice, originally made in 1906 by Charles Partridge of Stowbridge, Suffolk, who had previously donated to Dundee Libraries 81 letters, notes, and cards written by Mary Slessor to him in his position of District Commissioner in Calabar. Also included in his donation were four volumes written in the Efik language and her copy of the New Testament.[25] [26] [27]

In 1956, on a tour of Nigeria, Queen Elizabeth II intimated she would like to visit Slessor's grave. Her schedule was arranged to allow Her Majesty, accompanied by Prince Philip, to lay a wreath by the headstone. As the royal couple were driven around the area to acknowledge the crowds, thousands of schoolchildren and women performed ritual tribal dances for the occasion.[28] [29]

In 2000 she was chosen as one of the millennium persons of Calabar, the place she began her witness. She is honoured with statues, each a likeness of Slessor holding twin babies. A hospital, schools, and roads are named for her.

In 1997 she became the first Scottish woman to appear on a

Mary Mitchell Slessor Headstone
"The people that walked in darkness
Have seen a great light."
© *Mary Slessor Foundation.*

147

Scottish banknote when she was featured on the Clydesdale Bank ten-pound note. A bank spokesman said, "*We wanted a woman and after drawing up a shortlist … she was by far the best. Her extraordinary lifestyle revealed a woman who was really very unusual for her time*".[30]

On 2nd December 1998, 150 years after her birth, a plaque was unveiled by Aberdeen Lord Provost Margaret Farquhar at the Belmont Street entrance to the Academy Shopping Centre. This was the site of the former Belmont United Presbyterian Church, which Slessor attended as a child.[31]

In 2015, on the centenary of her death, a series of events were held throughout Dundee, including the unveiling of the granite Commemorative Standing Stone on 13th February at the Steeple Church. Commemorative plaques are installed at important locations featured in Mary Slessor's life.[32] The Mary Slessor Foundation, based in Calabar, was established to continue the work begun by Mary Slessor.

References

1   Douglas Binnie, Chair, Mary Slessor Foundation.
2   Ibid
3   *Arbroath Herald*, 10th December 1948, p. 12. col. 1.
4   *Dundee Evening Telegraph*, 21st September 1923, p. 7 col. 1.
5   *The Coming Day*, March 1917, p. 26 col. 2.
6   *Ibid*
7   Livingstone, WP, *Mary Slessor of Calabar, p. 44.*
8   Livingstone, WP, *Mary Slessor of Calabar, p. 51.*
9   *Aberdeen Press and Journal*, 26th November 1948, p. 2. col. 3.
10 *Brechin Advertiser*, 21st February 1956, p. 3. col. 1–2.
11 C. S. Lewis Institute. *Mary Slessor, Mother of all the Peoples*, p. 3.
12 *Free Suffrage Times*, 15th March 1917, p. 6. col. 2.
13 Douglas Binnie, Chair, *Mary Slessor Foundation.*
14 Enock, Esther E, *The Missionary Heroine of Calabar (London, 1937),* p. 66–67.
15 *The Coming Day*, March 1917, p. 26. col. 2.
16 Enock, Esther E, *The Missionary Heroine of Calabar,* p. 76–77.
17 Enock, Esther E, *The Missionary Heroine of Calabar,* p. 96.

18 C. S. Lewis Institute. https://www.cslewisinstitute.org

19 *Dundee Courier*, 18th July 1923, p. 5. col. 2.

20 *Dundee Evening Telegraph*, 16th October 1930, p. 2 col. 5.

21 *Dundee Courier*, 13th January 1936, p. 6. col. 3.

22 *Dundee Courier*, 29th September 1923, p. 3 col. 2.

23 *Dundee Courier*, 15th August 1939, p. 5. col. 3.

24 *Dundee Evening Telegraph*, 17th August 1939, p.6. col. 1.

25 *The Scotsman*, 12th September 1950, p. 3. col. 5.

26 *Dundee Courier,* 9th September 1953, p. 4. col.

27 *Dundee Courier*, 12th September 1953, p. 4 col. 4.

28 *Arbroath Herald*, 27th January 1956, p. 3. col. 1.

29 *Liverpool Echo*, 8th February 1956, p. 11. col. 5.

30 *Aberdeen Evening Express*, 4 July 1997, p. 31. col. 6.

31 *Aberdeen Evening Express*, 2nd December 1998, p. 21. col. 1.

32 Mary Slessor Centenary, *Programme of Events*. 2015.

Sir Alexander Grant
by Sir William Samuel Henry Llewellyn (EU0942)
© University of Edinburgh Art Collection.

Sir Alexander Grant

ALEXANDER Grant was born at 9 Bridge Street, Forres, Morayshire, on 1st October 1864, the eldest of nine children to Peter Grant and Elizabeth Norries. His father, a railway points-man, died when Grant was sixteen.[1]

Grant attended Forres Academy, leaving to find work in a solic-itor's office. This was a short-lived experience; when local baker Thomas Stuart offered Grant an apprenticeship, he leapt at the opportunity. On completion, Grant moved to a bakery in Inverness, where he stayed for some time, before heading to Edinburgh in 1887.

In Edinburgh, the young Grant talked himself into a job with Robert McVitie at his baker's shop in Rose Street.[2] McVitie's father had opened his first shop in Queensferry Street in the city and approximately 36 years later, his son, also Robert, returned from working in Europe, bringing his experience to the family shop.

There is an apocryphal story that the young Grant attended the McVitie offices every day for a week looking for employment, only to be told every day that there was no work for him. He per-severed, until one morning, he found himself sitting face-to-face with McVitie. After a chat, a disappointed Grant was once again rejected, but at the office door on his way out, he turned to McVitie and remarked, "*It's a pity you can't make biscuits*". Impressed with Grant's knowledge and enthusiasm, McVitie engaged the young Grant as an assistant. McVitie encouraged the ambitious Grant to attend Heriot-Watt College lectures on food chemistry and urged him to read all the published literature on modern baking technol-ogy he could find.

On 31st July 1887, Grant married Elizabeth Norris. The couple had three children, Robert, Elizabeth and Margaret. Still in his twenties, he was promoted to foreman. In experiments with ingredients in 1892, Grant found what he thought was a winning combination. Looking at the nutritional benefits, he decided that, as these biscuits would be beneficial to the digestive system, the name was obvious – the world-renowned digestive biscuit was born. By 1992, five million digestive biscuits were being eaten every day, produced from factories in Edinburgh, London and Manchester.

As a biscuit maker, the young McVitie traded from Merchant Street in the city; he acted as the travelling salesman, employing two bakers and an assistant in the shop. Less than two years later, he was joined by the ex-Member of Parliament for Central Edinburgh, Mr Charles Edward Price. An even more successful McVitie and Price built a new factory in Gorgie, on the west of the city.[3]

As fate would have it, a major fire forced the closure of the Edinburgh factory, relocating Grant as manager of the temporary replacement in Yorkshire. When the rebuilt Edinburgh factory opened, Grant returned to the city as manager. To cope with growing demand, a London factory began construction in November 1901.

In 1901, when CE Price retired, Grant was appointed general manager of the company. Nine years later, McVitie died childless and in June 1911, McVitie and Price was registered as a private limited company with Grant as Chairman and Managing Director.[4] In 1914, as the First World War was breaking out, they opened a further, more modern factory in Manchester, which was soon in full production supplying army and emergency ration biscuits for the government.

The new factory in Heaton Chapel, Manchester was a groundbreaking development, not only for the improvement and advances in the production of a huge range of products, but also in the treatment and care of workers, with Grant being described as an innovator and pioneer in workers' welfare. No more were workers confined to dark, airless spaces; departments were now "*... laid out on spacious lines, walls spotlessly white, high-domed roofs; light, airy, perfectly ventilated*". Areas were also added allowing workers to rest between shifts: "*There are well-furnished rest rooms, a medical department with resident trained nurses and bright cheerful dining rooms*", and cloakrooms which consisted of "*... huge grated enclosures in which coats etc are placed and locked. For the rest of the day they are subjected to currents of warm air, and in the evening when their owners require them again, they are perfectly dry*".

Neither did they ignore outdoor relaxation. With the purchase of land adjoining the factory, tennis courts, bowling greens, and the first golf course known to exist at a works premises were added. Similar welfare schemes existed at the Edinburgh and London factories, although restricted to availability of land.[5]

As time passed, Grant added a share bonus scheme, which accrued annually. The shares stayed with the employees for as long as they remained with the company, and the interest provided an income on retirement or for dependants on the death of the employee. Grant also initiated a scheme where the company provided up to a third of the money needed for one of their employees to buy their own house. This money was given as a gift, with no terms or conditions.[6]

The early 1920s was an extremely busy time for the company. Grant had become the majority shareholder, making him the head of the largest single-owned company in the country.

McVitie Price was now a hugely profitable company, allowing Grant to embark on a lifetime of charitable donations, beginning after the First World War when he cancelled the interest on £100,000 of war bonds held by the company, a decision which saved the Government £25,000. For comparison, £100,000 in 1918 had a spending power of approximately £5.75m in 2019.

In 1923 he donated £100,000 for the reconstituting of the Advocates Library in Edinburgh, which led to the establishment and endowment of the National Library of Scotland. The Chairman of the National Library Committee, Lord MacMillan, said that when Grant's banker handed him the cheque for the endowment, it was signed by Grant, but with a blank space left for MacMillan to complete. Grant donated a further sum of £100,000 in 1928 to assist with the construction of the library.[7]

He gifted Edinburgh University £100,000 for various projects, including clearing the debts caused by building projects, a sum which also included funds to build the Grant Institute of Geology, named in his honour and opened by his friend and fellow Moray man Ramsay MacDonald.[8]

In appreciation of his many contributions, he was awarded the Freedom of the City of Edinburgh in 1923.

In January 1923, James Ramsay MacDonald became prime minister. MacDonald's uncle and Grant's father had been friends since working together as guards on the Highland Railway. MacDonald was born and raised in Lossiemouth, close to Forres, and although at opposite ends of the political spectrum, the pair remained friends, regularly visiting each other through the years. MacDonald had no private income, and it shocked Grant to discover that, as prime minister, he was forced to travel to and from Downing Street, across London from his home in Hampstead, by underground. He felt it was *"Unreasonable that a man bearing such heavy burden should be forced to travel thus, inconveniently"*, declaring that his contribution to the prime minister's comforts should be a motor car.

MacDonald, uncomfortable with the offer, explained that he would have to be content with hiring one, as *"When he left office, he*

"Lady Elizabeth Bowes-Lyon being presented with a
bouquet when, with the Duke of York, she visited the
biscuit works of Messrs. McVitie and Price to decide upon
the design for her wedding cake."
From an original newspaper cutting, 22nd March 1923.

would likely be a poorer man than he was then". Even when Grant
explained he would endow it, MacDonald still declined, stating
that, *"As a man of simple habits, he had no desire to be the owner of a*
car". Grant persisted and, after several letter exchanges between the
pair, MacDonald agreed to his friend's offer. They agreed that the
car, a Daimler limousine, would be loaned to MacDonald, along
with McVitie shares to the value of £30,000, the interest on which
would pay for the upkeep and expenses of running the car.

The following year, 1924, he received a Baronetcy for public services,[9] causing an outcry in some newspapers suggesting that he received the Baronetcy in exchange for supplying the car and shares. MacDonald stated, "*The capital is not mine, and I only technically own the shares. The matter has nothing to do with politics. The arrangement was that a sum of money would be invested in my name and the income from it I was to enjoy during my lifetime so long as I kept a car.*"[10]

In a later interview he again reiterated Grant's donation of the car was a simple act of kindness, "*Sir Alexander Grant got his Baronetcy for public services, including the gift of the National Library to Scotland, of which most people know, and for which he has received the freedom of Edinburgh*".

When the news of the Baronetcy was announced, the Duke of York publicly praised Grant: "*I feel that my special and intimate knowledge of your valuable and generous activities justifies me in sending you this expression of my congratulations. Your good works ungrudgingly performed and your well-known interest in all that concerns the welfare and happiness of your workpeople have long merited this recognition. Yours very sincerely, Albert.*"

In November, just two months after receiving the car, MacDonald resigned from his position as prime minister, also announcing that following his resignation he had decided to relinquish all interests in the shares which were transferred to him by Grant.[11]

In the same year, the University of Edinburgh conferred Grant with an Honorary Doctor of Laws Degree.

In 1924 Grant purchased the highland country sporting estate of Logie,[12] shortly afterward adding the adjoining estate of Relugas. The combined estates boast some of the finest salmon fishing in Scotland. Three generations of his descendants currently live on the estate. The latest is the sixth generation of Sir Alexander's family to live at Logie.[13] On the 17th June 1929, shortly after MacDonald's second term as prime minister, Grant placed his highland home at the service of MacDonald and his government for a historic meeting with General Dawes, the American ambassador, to discuss naval disarmament between both countries.[14]

In 1924 Grant donated £5,000 to the Scottish Federation of Grocers and Provision Merchants' Association to institute a benevolent fund for the good of their members.

Grant never forgot his upbringing and made many generous donations in his home town of Forres. As well as supplying various cups and awards for local clubs and teams, he paid for a motorised fire engine, complete with the most modern equipment (1930), and gifted four stained-glass windows to Forres Parish Church (1931). He made a £26,000 interest-free loan to Nairn town's harbour scheme, a £5,000 donation for the redevelopment of the town's public baths and also subsidised Lossiemouth golf course.[15]

On 27th August 1932, he was made a Freeman of Forres; his friend Ramsay MacDonald attended the ceremony. After lunch and toasts, the company moved to Grant Park, where Lady Grant made the formal opening of both Grant Park and the new bowling green within its grounds. Both had recently been donated to the town by Grant and the couple stated they were 'at home', making themselves available to meet the many members of the public who attended. In the same year, he was also made a Freeman of Nairn.[16]

In 1935, in celebration of George V's Silver Jubilee, Grant made a gift of 30,500 caskets of biscuits; each casket bearing a portrait of the king and queen. It took 10 workers 25 days at the McVitie and Price Edinburgh factory to prepare the donation.

Grant also provided the Palace of Holyroodhouse with a silver banqueting service, at an estimated cost of £10,000. The service provided for 100 people and contained over 4,000 items. Engraved by hand on each piece is the royal crest, while the silver salvers and trays bear the full insignia of the royal arms. All the pieces were manufactured in Scotland. As an addition, Grant also provided 7,000 items of linen, woven in Dunfermline. When first announced, shortly after the coronation, the donor's name was not disclosed, but it was later revealed that Grant had given the gift as a memorial to the Silver Jubilee of King George V.[17]

Previously, when a monarch travelled to Edinburgh, the banqueting service and linen from Buckingham Palace had to be packed into crates and transported to Scotland's capital by train. Grant said that he had hoped the gift would encourage the king and queen to visit Scotland on a more regular basis. The service and linen were put on public display at the Scottish National Gallery on 17th May 1937 for three weeks.

Grant developed a chill after attending the coronation of George VI at Westminster Abbey on 12th May 1937. By the time he returned home to Scotland, the 'chill' had developed into something much more serious and a doctor was summoned. George VI's personal physician, Lord Horner, travelled from London to diagnose an advanced stage of lumbar pneumonia.[18]

Sir Alexander Grant died on Friday 21st May 1937, age 72, in the family home at 15 Hermitage Drive, Morningside, Edinburgh with Lord Horner in attendance.[19] [20]

One of the first messages of condolence arrived by telegram from Buckingham Palace stating, "*The Queen and I are much grieved to hear of the death of our old friend and send you our deep sympathy in your sad loss. (signed) George R.I.*"[21]

Fulsome tributes were paid by many, including Ramsay MacDonald, who said, "*... His gift to the National Library of Scotland was one of the most patriotic of offerings given to the country of his birth and his love, for he was a great Scotsman. Only those who*

The official wedding cake presented to Princess Elizabeth.
From an original newspaper cutting.

have known him intimately know what his death means, I can hardly yet believe the news".[22]

Sir Alexander Grant's funeral, in Clunyhill Cemetery, Forres was one of the largest seen in the North of Scotland, with streets lined from the Church of St Laurence to the graveside.[23]

In Grant's will, Grant never forgot his friend, bequeathing MacDonald the income of £40,000 for the remainder of his life. Sadly, MacDonald passed away barely six months later while on holiday, on board the ocean liner *Reina del Pacifico* on 9th November 1937.[24]

After her husband's death, Lady Grant continued to support philanthropic activities to the benefit of the people of Forres. In addition to making several donations to Forres Academy and the Forres and District Nursing Association, she donated £17,000 for the construction of a maternity wing at Leanchoil Hospital in the town. Lady Grant passed away after a short illness on Sunday 28th April 1940 at the family home.

Grant's son, who inherited his baronetcy, became Sir Robert McVitie Grant on the death of his father, and the heir to the McVitie Price business. Sir Robert continued with the family ethos, contributing to the town of Forres when he purchased and donated Muiryshade Golf Course to the townspeople in 1945. Tragically, Sir Robert died in 1947, leaving no direct heir.

His sisters both married sons of Hector Laing, a fish merchant in the city. Elizabeth married Herbert Stanley Laing in 1921, and the following year Margaret married Hector Laing. Unfortunately, Elizabeth died in Eastbourne in 1927. Margaret, as the sole surviving sibling, became heir to the McVitie fortune.

In 1947 McVitie continued the family support of the Monarch, by making the wedding cake celebrating the marriage of future Queen, Princess Elizabeth and Philip Mountbatten. In a Britain still under rationing, the ingredients for the 9ft-tall cake were flown to Britain from South Africa and Australia.

In April 2011, future King, Prince William chose a 'Groom's Cake' made from 1,700 McVitie's rich tea biscuits and over 17kg of chocolate, for his wedding to Catherine Middleton.

When Sir Robert died in 1947, he had already begun a transformation of the business when he instigated a merger with McFarlane, Lang and Co, a prominent biscuit manufacturer based in Glasgow. The following year, now led by Peter McDonald, former legal advisor to the company, negotiations were concluded and United Biscuits was formed.

Margaret's husband Hector Laing became managing director of the company on McDonald's retirement and led United Biscuits until his son, also Hector, became Chairman in 1972. Lord Laing of Dunphail, as he became known, steered the company through a period of extraordinary growth before he retired as chairman in 1990.

However, the following decade saw sales fall worldwide leading the company vulnerable to a takeover bid and, in 2000, United Biscuits was sold to investment group Finalrealm for a reported £1.26bn.

In 2014 the company was sold to Turkish food group Yildiz for £2bn, becoming part of subsidiary group, Pladis in 2016.

It had been widely reported that Sir Alexander Grant's great-great-grandson, and star of reality television show *Made in Chelsea*, Jamie Laing, is heir to the McVitie fortune. However, in a series of interviews in November 2020, Laing claimed he was not the heir. It was thought that his father had sold his shares in the company in the mid-90s. Laing is quoted, "*We sold the company a long time ago, but I don't know where that money went. I haven't seen any of it. It's pretty upsetting. I'm hoping one day I find it. I don't even get free biscuits.*"[25]

In 2012, along with friend and fellow student Ed Williams, Laing founded the vegan confectionery company, Candy Kittens[26]. A crowdfunding campaign in 2015 raised £300,000, but the company decided to return the money raised favouring an investment by an individual, enabling domestic expansion. In 2019 German confectioner Katjes Group announced a further investment in Candy Kittens, taking their total investment to "more than 50%" of the share capital, aiming for a projected worldwide turnover of £50m in the near future.[27]

Jamie Laing's great-great-grandfather would have been delighted that such entrepreneurship still runs in the family.

References

1   *National Records of Scotland.* Births.
2   *The Independent.* https://www.independent.co.uk/news/obituaries
3   *Westminster Gazette,* 15th October 1925, p. 2.
4   *Westminster Gazette,* 15th October 1925, p. 4.
5   *Westminster Gazette,* 15th October 1925, p. 5.
6   *Westminster Gazette,* 15th October 1925, p. 8.
7   *Gloucester Journal,* 7th July 1928, p. 18. col. 1.
8   *Gazetteer for Scotland.* https://www.scottish-places.info
9   *Edinburgh Evening News,* 3rd June 1924, p. 7. col. 1–2.
10 *Exeter and Plymouth Gazette,* 13th September 1924, p.8 col. 2.
11 *The Western Morning News,* 3rd November 1924, p. 5. col. 3.
12 *Northern Whig,* 20th September 1924, p. 9. col. 5.
13 *The Logie Estate.* https://www.logie.co.uk/estate/family-history/
14 *Sheffield Independent,* 26th February 1931, p. 6. col. 6.
15 *University of St Andrews,* Centre for the Study of Philanthropy and Good.
16 *Aberdeen Press and Journal,* 12th August 1924, p. 1. col. 7.
17 *Nottingham Evening Post,* 17th May 1927, p. 5. col. 2.
18 *Sunderland Daily Echo,* 17th May 1937, p. 6. col. 1.
19 *Portsmouth Evening News,* 21st May 1937, p. 1.3 col. 2.
20 *Hull Daily News,* 21st May 1937, p. 1. col. 3.
21 *Western Daily Press,* 22nd May 1937, p. 7. col. 2.

22 *Nottingham Evening Post,* 21st May 1937, p. 9. col. 4.

23 *The Scotsman,* 26th May 1937, p. 16. col. 4.

24 *Western Gazette,* 4th June 1937, p. 12. col. 2.

25 *Oxfordshirelive.* https://www.oxfordshirelive.co.uk

26 *Real Business.* https://www.realbusiness.co.uk

27 *Confectionery News,* https://www.confectionerynews.com

Flora MacDonald.
by Alan Ramsay. 1749.
From Bonnie Prince Charlie by Clennell Wilkinson.
Harrap & Co. 1932.

Flora MacDonald

FLORA Macdonald was born at Milton, on the island of South Uist, Outer Hebrides in 1722. The day and month of her birth are unknown. She was the daughter of Ranald MacDonald, a tacksman (or farmer), and his second wife, Marion. Flora had two older brothers, Angus, who would eventually inherit the Milton farm, and Ranald, who died in an accident as a young man.

The family was not poor; a tacksman could farm the land himself, or rent it, or parts of it, to other members of the clan. He controlled the tack at both Milton and Balivanich, which gave the family considerable respect in the community. This indicated that he would also have been well placed in the MacDonald clan. Flora's mother had a connection to the MacDonalds of Sleat, who were known as the Lords of the Isles.

Ranald MacDonald died when Flora was two years old, and four years later her mother married Hugh MacDonald of Armadale. By reputation, he had lived a life of adventure. A fearsome swordsman, he was known as Uisdean Cam, or One-Eyed Hugh, as he had lost an eye, either in his youth, or as an officer in the French Army.

After her marriage, Marion relocated to Skye with her new husband and indicated that she wanted to take the six-year-old Flora with her. However, Angus, now successfully managing Milton, felt she should stay with him at what had always been her family home. Ultimately, it was left to Flora to choose. She quickly decided that as she did not know Skye, and did not care for it, she would stay at Milton because she loved it there.[1]

The young Flora was popular with many of the families on South Uist, resulting in her spending a lot of time away from the farm and in long stays with other relatives. However she seldom left South Uist save for short visits to see her mother. Lady Clanranald, wife of the clan chieftain, took the young Flora under her wing, at times acting more as a mother than a distant relative.

The islanders regarded education as important and it was well organised. Teachers were brought from the mainland to look after their pupils at various locations on the island. When Flora was about 13, it is said that Lady Clanranald insisted she came to stay with her at the family mansion at Nunton on Benbecula, providing her with the benefit of a governess who was already looking after her own children.

It is often suggested that Flora received her education in Edinburgh; however, Flora is herself on record as saying that she never left Skye until the age of 22. Regardless of the manner of her education, by 1745 she was a young woman of 23, well versed in Gaelic culture, songs and music, and she played the spinet beautifully.

In his book of 1747, *The Lyon in Mourning*, Robert Forbes describes Flora, "*She is of a low stature, of a fair complexion and well enough shap'd. One could not discern by her conversation that she had spent all her former days in the Highlands; for she talks English (or rather Scots) easily, and not at all through the Earse tone. She has a sweet voice and sings well; and no lady, Edinburgh bred, can acquit herself better at the tea table ... She is the delight of her friends and the envy of her enemies*".

Equally, when James Boswell paid her a visit, as described in his celebrated *Journal of a Tour to the Hebrides* of 1773, he describes Flora, "*She is a little woman, of a genteel appearance, and uncommonly mild and well-bred*".

In the early part of 1745, Flora, after spending some weeks on Skye with her mother and stepfather, returned to South Uist, and

MAP OF SCOTLAND

Scotland.
From Bonnie Prince Charlie.
Published by Harrap & Co. 1932

found an island awash with rumour and counter-rumour of an imminent Jacobite rebellion. The Stuarts' strongest support lay in South Uist, where many hoped the rebellion would commence.

The 1745 Jacobite Rebellion did indeed begin in the islands of Uist when a French ship landed Prince Charles Edward Stuart on Eriskay on 23rd July. His aim was to overthrow King George II and claim the thrones of England, Ireland and Scotland, thus restoring the Stuart dynasty, who had been forced into exile in France.

Despite victories in earlier battles of the campaign, the '45 Rebellion was a disaster for the Jacobite cause. A tired, malnourished, and ill-equipped body of 5,000 men faced 8,000 highly equipped and well-prepared men of the Duke of Cumberland on the battlefield at Culloden on 16th April. It quickly became a rout by Cumberland's men; in less than an hour, at least 1,200 Jacobites lay dead, while the English counted only 50 of their number. As battle raged, Prince Charles Edward's commanders quickly realised that their position was hopeless and, despite his protestations, led him from the battlefield to begin his flight to safety.

The repercussions in Scotland were severe; the country was put under martial law with promises of torture awaiting those Jacobites captured. Jacobite Lords Kilmarnock and Balmerino were beheaded, and 3,500 suspected Jacobites captured. Of these, almost a thousand were executed or died awaiting trial, with 1,500 transported. Upwards of 2,000 of Cumberland's redcoats ravaged the country in their search for Prince Charles Edward, burning whole towns and villages to the ground. Men, women and children were slaughtered in what is now seen by many as an act of genocide against the Highland people, an act which earned Prince William, the youngest son of George II, the title of 'Butcher Cumberland'.[2]

Prince Charles Edward, by this time travelling with only two trusted companions, Captain Felix O'Neil and Neil MacEachain, spent the following two months evading capture. Given the damage to the country and its people, support from the clan chiefs was split. Certainly, any sign of support for the Jacobite cause would see instant arrest. In addition, a £30,000 reward put on his head tested the loyalty of even his most stalwart supporter.

Advised by O'Neil that the prince could more easily find a ship to France in the Western Isles than the mainland, the trio made their way cross-country to the Hebrides. It was a dangerous time for Prince Charles Edward. Plagued by bad weather, their journey took them over many of the islands until he found himself back on South Uist, close to where the venture began.

O'Neil, aware Flora was on the island visiting her brother at Milton and that she visited her mother on Skye, contrived to meet her[3]. He explained to Flora he was sure her stepfather would furnish her with a pass. It is thought by many that even though he was a captain of the militia, Hugh, in his former role as a soldier in France, was already acquainted with O'Neil. Flora herself said her stepfather met and shook the hand of Prince Charles Edward when he first landed in South Uist. It is very likely that it was Hugh, while carrying out his clan obligations to wear the uniform of the crown, who came up with the plan for the prince's escape.

They devised a simple plan.[4] Flora was to pay her mother a visit in Skye, taking the prince with her, disguised as a servant, a spinster woman. With too much that could go wrong, Flora immediately declined. She told O'Neil that it would grieve her more if the prince was captured while in her care than any other way. At this, O'Neil called in Prince Charles Edward himself, who was in hiding close by. The prince assured Flora that he would furnish her with the pass, to which Flora replied that she feared her reputation would be ruined if she was to be in such close company with the prince and himself.

Prince Charles (The Pretender) and Flora MacDonald.
From an original print c1838.
The London Printing and Publishing Company.
© Jerry Brannigan

O'Neil responded gallantly by offering to marry her, then and there, in a traditional handfasting ceremony.[5] Flora disavowed him of this notion. At that, the prince, almost begging, made a sincere appeal to her sense of duty, for Scotland, and its people. Still protesting the dangers, Flora relented and agreed to the prince's wishes, but only on condition that the pass was secured.

While Prince Charles Edward took to the hills, Flora set out for Lady Clanranald's home, only to be stopped by a party of local militia and, as she had no pass to be out, she was taken into custody. Flora asked to see their commanding officer, to be told that he was not there, but the officer in charge was Captain (Hugh) MacDonald. On hearing this, she realised she had no alternative but to wait. On his return in the morning, Hugh appeared surprised to see Flora but showed no concern at her request for a pass for herself, a manservant called Neil MacEachain, and her Irish maid Betty Burke. Further, she entreated him to recommend Burke, an excellent spinster, by means of a letter to her mother, as she knew her mother would appreciate such a person greatly. As they spoke, the guards brought MacEachain forward. The prince had sent him in search of Flora in the night and the militia had intercepted and arrested him. Hugh asked no more, supplying the pass and letter, allowing Flora and MacEachain to leave.[6]

Flora immediately went to Lady Clanranald, repeating the earlier events.[7] Without question, Lady Clanranald immediately gathered the women of the house to set about adapting and manufacturing the clothes that would allow a full-grown man to pass for a *"counterfeit lady spinster"*, complete with large hooded cloak.

When Flora returned to Prince Charles Edward and O'Neil, he dressed himself in his disguise and they set off for Skye. The prince suggested he should take a pistol, secreted on his body, but Flora said no; if they were to meet soldiers, they may be searched. The

The Western Islands
From Bonnie Prince Charlie.
Published by Harrap & Co. 1932.

prince replied, "*Indeed, Miss, if we shall happen to meet with any that will go so narrowly to work in searching as what you mean they will certainly discover me at any rate.*"[8]

Perhaps the huge reward for Prince Charles Edward's head generated information as the area was suddenly swarming with 1,500 redcoats.[9] Two Royal Navy warships – one of which, the HMS *Furnace*, with the hated Captain Ferguson on board – sat at either end of the channel. Ferguson was responsible for many atrocities in the Highlands, making this an even more precarious journey.

They set off around eight o'clock in the evening, when there was little light left. The prince, making an effort to put everyone at ease, sang Jacobite songs, and with good humour encouraged the oarsmen to join in as they worked. The sea was wild in the night, although this didn't prevent them from being seen. Shots were fired in their direction, but despite the rough water they managed to manoeuvre the boat along the coast. Amongst the rocks they went unnoticed, giving the rowers time to recover. After the contact with the redcoats, they realised that the government forces would try to track their boat's progress along the coast, but in the darkness, after several failures to land, they finally found a safe spot near to Monkstadt, the family seat of Sir Alexander MacDonald and his wife, Lady Margaret.

Flora set off to the home of Sir Alexander, only to find him away. His wife, though somewhat flustered, was not completely surprised by the sudden appearance of Flora. The timing of her arrival could have been better, for at that moment, sitting at Lady Margaret's dinner table was a small gathering of local guests, including her factor Alexander MacDonald of Kingsburgh, known as Kingsburgh, and Captain MacLeod, who with his company of militia were in the area searching for the prince.

While Lady Margaret made an excuse, Flora sat at the dining

table and engaged Captain MacLeod in chat about his hunt for the prince.[10] James Boswell wrote in his *Journal of a Tour to the Hebrides* that Flora recounted this story often, laughing in good humour with this officer gentleman, on her "*... having so well deceived him*".

As dinner was being served, Kingsburgh made his way to the hiding place in the hills with food and the news that, for Prince Charles Edward's safety, they would go to his home that same evening. At Kingsburgh, the party received a joyous welcome, and despite the danger, allowed the prince to sleep under the family roof. It had already been decided, as soon as possible thereafter, the prince would travel to Portree where a boat could take him safely from South Uist.

The following morning, Flora, concerned that rumour of the prince disguised in female attire would spread, said that the prince should leave the house in the same dress that he arrived in, swapping it for a hidden set of clothes some distance from the house. The prince was not a particularly convincing woman. Not only younger, taller and stronger than the typical spinster, he was most ungainly in walking, taking large strides, holding his skirts too far up his legs as he moved, creating great scandal. One of the children at Kingsburgh, on seeing this spinster maid in the house, ran to her mother saying "*... my father has brought in a very odd, muckle, ill-shapen-up wife, as ever I saw, I never saw the like o' her*". MacEachain said of the prince that he was the "*... worst pretender he had ever seen*".[11]

While the prince travelled over the hills with a trusted guide, Flora, on horseback with MacEachain, arrived at Portree some time before him. MacEachain, who had grown up in the area, soon found the owner of a boat in the local inn who was willing to take the prince to the Island of Raasay and to comparative safety. In the early hours of Tuesday 1st July, Prince Charles Edward and Flora said their goodbyes as he set out for Raasay.

Having taken leave of the prince, Flora left Portree and returned to Lady Margaret, where she intended to stay for some time. Within days, Flora was arrested and taken on board the *Furnace*. Fortunately for Flora, General Campbell was on board and questioned her himself with respect, compassion and some curiosity for the situation in which she found herself. On hearing that the rowers had been captured and had confessed, Flora acknowledged to Campbell the truth in her part of the endeavour. It is likely she would have based her answers on the information the rowers would have been able to give.

Flora remained calm, on the exterior anyway; inside, she must have been terrified. Author Hugh Douglas suggests that as experienced soldiers, Captain O'Neil and MacEachain would likely have discussed the possibility of capture with Flora and how she should behave. Robert Forbes writes that while O'Neil was also a prisoner on the prison ship *Bridgewater* at anchor in Leith, he fleetingly met Flora on board. She gently slapped his face with the back of her hand saying, "*... it is to this face that I owe all my misfortune*". Smiling, he replied, "*Why, Madam, what you call your misfortune is truly your greatest honour*", continuing "*... if you be careful to demean yourself agreeably to the character you have already acquired, you will in the event find it to be your happiness. ... be not frighten'd by the thoughts of your present circumstances either to say or do anything that may in the least tend to contradict or sully the character you are now mistress of*".[12]

Forbes also writes of O'Neil, when imprisoned in Edinburgh Castle, telling those who visited him he had felt the same pains as any parent would have with a child, laying down rules for Flora in her future behaviour if she had the misfortune to become a prisoner.

Impressed with her calm demeanour and apparent honesty, General Campbell commanded the lady be treated with the utmost civility, that she should be allowed a maid-servant and as fine accommodation as was available.

When the ship was passing near the home of her mother, true to his word, Campbell permitted Flora to go ashore to say goodbye, on condition that a guard remained with her at all times and she did not speak Gaelic. He also permitted her to take on board the young Kate MacDonald as her maid and companion. It must have been an emotional farewell to her mother; no one knew what future, if any, lay before her.

Taken to Dunstaffnage Castle, near Oban, Flora was detained as a special prisoner. Her fame travelled before her; barely a day had passed before she began to receive calls from "... *all respectable families in the neighbourhood*".

After only a few days at Dunstaffnage, Flora was taken aboard the HMS *Eltham*, the ship of Commodore Smith, and joined a convoy of five Royal Navy ships, each loaded with prisoners, returning to Leith.

The *Eltham* arrived in Leith on 16th September, transferring Flora to the prison ship HMS *Bridgewater*, where she remained for two months. In Leith, Flora was allowed visitors and quickly became a celebrity with the ladies of Edinburgh. Lady Bruce, the 67-year-old Jacobite supporter and leader of society in the city, befriended Flora and visited often, bringing gifts such as cloth, threads and needles. Her visitors were, in the main, young ladies enthralled by romantic stories of Flora's escapade with the "*Highland hero, Bonnie Prince Charlie*". They came every day to listen, captivated by Flora repeating the same story time and again.

When the *Bridgewater* left Leith bound for London, large crowds gathered to cheer and wave as the ship sailed away to an uncertain future in the English capital.

On 6th December 1746, Flora arrived in London, highly

commended by both General Campbell and Commodore Smith that she should receive special treatment as a lady of society.[13] As a result, she was confined to a messenger's house. *The Derby Mercury* described her as "*... a young person of some fortune in the Highlands, and affects great humanity and benevolence, has certainly a good share of sense, and her deportment is very modest and reserved*".[14]

Again, she was allowed visitors and, as in Edinburgh, her celebrity status brought influential people. London Jacobite, Lady Primrose, who was very taken with Flora, soon befriended her and began a subscription, raising the huge sum of £1,500 by the time she had been freed.

The king's son, Prince Frederick visited Flora, curious to see the woman, an apparent royalist, who had helped their enemy escape, On asking her the question, Flora replied she acted out of compassion for someone in trouble and if the roles were reversed, and if it was himself, the son of the king asking for help, she would have acted in the same way.

Without being asked any questions relating to Prince Charles Edward, Flora was released under a general amnesty to those captured after Culloden. *The Caledonian Mercury* of 13th April 1747 reported that as workmen were beginning to build the scaffold on Tower Hill for the execution of Lord Lovat, several ladies "*... who were taken up on account of the late rebellion are ordered to be discharged ... including Miss Flora MacDonald*". On her release, Flora travelled to Edinburgh, where she spent the winter, before returning to Skye in April 1748. She stayed in Skye for several weeks before travelling back to London and Lady Primrose, it is thought, to sort out her finances.[15]

On 6th November 1750, Flora married Allan MacDonald of Kingsburgh, son of Alexander MacDonald of Kingsburgh, who had played his part in the escape of Prince Charles Edward. They had seven children: Charles, Anne, Alexander, Ranald, James, John and Frances. They farmed at Flodigarry on Skye, and although Kingsburgh was keen, he had little business sense. The farm, or more likely Kingsburgh, quickly used up Flora's fortune, leaving them financially broken.[16]

Boswell described Kingsburgh on their first meeting: *"Kingsburgh was completely the figure of a gallant Highlander, exhibiting 'the graceful mien, the manly looks,' which our popular Scots song has justly attributed to the character. He has his Tartan plaid thrown about him, a large blue bonnet with a knot of black ribbon like a cockade, a brown short coat of a kind of duffil, a Tartan waistcoat with gold buttons and gold button-holes, a bluish philibeg, and Tartan hose. He had jet black hair tied behind, and was a large stately man, with a steady, sensible countenance. ... Yet in reality my heart was grieved when I recollected that Kingsburgh was embarrassed in his affairs, and intended to go to America."* [17] [18]

Like the thousands of highlanders whose lives were devastated because of the repercussions of the '45 Rebellion, Flora and Kingsburgh emigrated to America, travelling in 1774 to Cheeks Creek, North Carolina, where there was an established community of highlanders.[19]

When the American War of Independence broke out in 1755, Kingsburgh, who had been an officer in the army of King George II in Scotland, remained true to his support of the British Government.[20] He joined the Royal Highland Emigrants 84th Regiment, where he became a lieutenant colonel. As a high-ranking officer, he used Flora's reputation and influence to raise a force of fellow highlanders, many of them his neighbours, in support of the king. This was one of his poorer decisions.

On their first foray into battle with the congressmen on 27th February 1776, Kingsburgh's regiment came with too few men and even fewer weapons; claymores were no match for bullets.[21] As at Culloden, it was a disaster; however, on this occasion, the defeat was for the forces of the Crown. Saboteurs removed planks from a bridge, leaving Kingsburgh's men trapped and ripe for ambush. Under a barrage of fire, many highlanders were immediately killed or wounded, leaving the bloodied survivors with no alternative but to surrender. The engagement, known as *The Battle of Moore's Creek Bridge*, had lasted only a matter of 20 minutes. Kingsburgh, and other captive officers were forced to walk from post to post for the 700 miles to Philadelphia, where they were imprisoned for two years.[22]

In the meantime, when news arrived back in the township that many men had either been killed or taken prisoner, their wives and children turned on Flora, who was already ill with a fever.

She became a target for stragglers from the battle, openly helping themselves to her property. Such was the ill-feeling against her that even her servants left her. Abandoned and in despair, with the farm destroyed and every item stolen, Flora had no option but to stay with her daughter, whose husband had also been captured.

When the fever broke and her health improved, Flora tried to visit the wives of some men who had been taken prisoner. On one of these visits, she fell from her horse, breaking her right arm. As the only doctor in the area was a prisoner with her husband, she remained in this condition, making the best she could of her situation while waiting for Allan's return.

Over two years after Kingsburgh had headed off to war, opposing forces struck a short truce, allowing Flora and her children to travel to New York City, which was still in the hands of the British. There she could join Kingsburgh,[23] who had now been released. She remained for some time in New York where Kingsburgh commanded a company of volunteers, all of them Scottish, before his transfer to a regiment in Halifax, Nova Scotia. Still delicate in her recovery, the pair travelled to Windsor in the Bay of Minas, a journey that took five days through snow covered countryside and into a winter so cold that if it were not for the sake of the regiment, they would surely have starved.

The following summer, Flora fell and dislocated the wrist of her left hand, damaging tendons; and although she had the aid of the Regimental Surgeon, she was still indisposed for two months. Her long recovery made her increasingly homesick and depressed until eventually Kingsburgh found her a berth in late 1779 on the *Lord Dunsmore*, a ship of 24 guns, to return to Scotland. In the open sea, the ship was forced to make emergency manoeuvres to evade contact with a French gunship. In the hurry to get below deck, Flora slipped on the stair, fell and broke the already dislocated arm. The arm was set with pieces of wood, but the incident confined Flora to bed until their arrival in London.[24]

In London she received distressing news: her son Alexander's ship was missing, presumed lost while travelling home. This news brought the already fragile Flora even lower, leading to a six-month recuperation in London. In May 1780 she travelled to Edinburgh to meet John MacKenzie,[25] to whom she had entrusted the care of her son John, now 20 years old. While the other sons served with the army and navy in America, John initially served as a cadet with the Bengal Engineers before promotion as a surveyor.[26]

On her journey back to South Uist, Flora visited her daughter, Anne, at Dunvegan Castle; she was so ill that Anne refused to allow her to travel any farther. Flora stayed at Dunvegan Castle or with friends and relatives on the island for a further three years while she waited on Kingsburgh's return. During this time, Flora received more devastating news. In late 1782 Ranald, serving in the Royal Navy, was lost when his ship floundered off Newfoundland.

Kingsburgh returned to Skye in 1785. Life had taken a heavy toll on both Flora and her husband, now well into their sixties and, troubled by poor health, they never left the island again. They had departed America in near poverty, however, thanks to their son John they were able to live the rest of their lives in some comfort.

When John left Edinburgh University, he gained a cadetship with the East India Company, and established his expertise as a surveyor, quickly moving through the ranks until he was made lieutenant-colonel. As a surveyor, his maps of St Helena and Sumatra can be found in the collections of the British Museum. He was made a Fellow of the Royal Society in 1800, and wrote many books on a variety of diverse subjects including surveying, engineering and infantry tactics. Having made his fortune in the East, he retired at 41.

In October 1789, shortly before her death, Flora recalled an account of her time in North Carolina and Nova Scotia in a letter to Sir John MacPherson.[27] For many years, Flora had suffered from regular bouts of depression and pain from her injuries; unable to write, she dictated and signed the paper. It ended …

"The casts in both my arms are living monuments of my suffering and distress and the long goal confinement which my husband under-went has brought on such disorders that he has totally lost the use of both of his legs …"

They spent their last years at home on Skye, with four of their five surviving children living nearby.

Flora MacDonald died at Penduin, near Kingsburgh, Skye on 4th March 1790. She is buried in the graveyard at Kilmuir. Legend tells us that her body was wrapped in a shroud made from the bed-sheets Prince Charles Edward lay on when he slept through the night at the home of Sir Alexander and Lady Margaret MacDonald. More than 3,000 people attended her funeral, at which it is said 300 gallons of whisky were drunk.

Flora MacDonald's Grave. Kilmuir. Skye.
© Jerry Brannigan.

Her husband Allan died two years later on 20th September 1792.

Originally, her grave was marked with a simple stone, but John later organised a fine marble panel to cover the grave. Damaged on installation, as Jacobite supporters arrived to pay homage to her life over the years, they took small pieces of the panel as mementos until no panel remained. In 1871 a Celtic cross on a tall marble stem was erected, but the winds in this exposed position proved too strong and in 1880, a replacement cross was built, this time with iron straps to give additional security.

During the time when Flora was in London in 1747, her portrait was painted by Richard Wilson and is now part of the collection at the National Portrait Gallery. It is suggested Wilson made several portraits of Flora, intending to use them as the basis for engravings which were then used by Jacobite supporters.

In 1749 Alan Ramsay painted Flora in all her Jacobean finery of tartan shawl and white roses. It is to be found in the Ashmolean Museum, University of Oxford.

On Skye, a stained-glass window commemorating Flora's life was dedicated in 1896 in Portree Episcopal Church.

At Inverness, a statue was erected in 1899 to honour Flora, who stands looking out towards the islands.[28]

The Skye Boat Song was published in 1869 and is an amalgam of an old tune sung by sailors and new words by Miss Annie MacLeod and Harold Boulton. Flora has a mention in passing; however, this is no love song, but a view of the aftermath of the '45 rebellion.

Skye Boat Song

Speed, Bonnie boat, like a bird on the wing
Onward, the sailors cry!
carry the lad that's born to be King
Over the sea to Skye.

Loud the winds howl, loud the waves roar,
Thunderclaps rend the air;
Baffled our foes stand by the shore,
Follow they do not dare.

Many's the lad fought on that day
Well the claymore could wield,
When the night came silently lay
Dead on Culloden field

Though the waves leap, soft shall ye sleep,
Ocean's a royal bed.
Rocked in the deep, Flora will keep
watch by your weary head.

Burned are their homes, exile and death
Scatter the loyal men;
Yet, ere the sword cool in the sheath
Charlie will come again.

Annie MacLeod and Harold Boulton

Flora MacDonald

References

1   Electric Scotland, *Women of History of Scots Descent*, Flora Macdonald.
2   *Scots Magazine*, October 1773. *Emigrations to America from the Highland and Islands*. (NLS Sc. Mag.)
3   *Bradford Observer*, 2nd August 1873, p. 7. col. 1–2.
4   The National Archives (NA), *Flora Macdonald's statement on the escape of Charles Edward Stewart from South Uist (Outer Hebrides) to Skye*, on 12 July 1746. (SP 54/32 f.49E)
5   Douglas, Hugh, *Flora Macdonald, The Most Loyal Rebel*, (Sutton. 2003) p. 27.
6   *Montrose Standard and Angus Mearns Register*, 29th June 1849.
7   *NA, Flora Macdonald's statement on the escape of Charles Edward Stewart.*
8   Forbes, Robert. *The Lyon in Mourning*, Vol 1, 1895, (NLS shelfmark SCS. SHS. 20-SCS. SHS. 22) p. 111.
9   *Scotsman*, 29th November 1938, *Flora Macdonald's narrative of Prince Charles Edward's escape.*
10 *NA, Flora Macdonald's statement on the escape of Charles Edward Stewart.*
11 Boswell's *Journal of a Tour to the Hebrides with Samuel Johnson* (London, 1773) (NLS. DNC23 1852) P. 147.
12 Forbes, Robert. *The Lyon in Mourning*, NLS. Vol 1, 1895, p. 113.
13 Douglas, Hugh, *Flora Macdonald, The Most Loyal Rebel*, p. 84.
14 *Boswell's Journal of a Tour to the Hebrides with Samuel Johnson* P. 143.
15 *Boswell's Journal of a Tour to the Hebrides with Samuel Johnson* P. 157.
16 *Brave Sons of Skye*, (Edinburgh, 1899) (NLS, shelfmark: S121. c)
17 *Boswell's Journal of a Tour to the Hebrides with Samuel Johnson* P. 142.
18 *Boswell's Journal of a Tour to the Hebrides with Samuel Johnson* P. 143.
19 (*NLS*, shelfmark: S121. c)
20 *North Carolina History*, https://northcarolinahistory.org/encyclopedia/flora-macdonald-1722-1790/
21 (*NLS*, Shelfmark: S121. c)
22 *History of American Women*, https://www.womenhistoryblog.com/2009/04/flora-macdonald.html
23 Flora MacDonald on their time in Nova Scotia. (NLS shelfmark: MS. 2681, ff 82–84)
24 *Boswell's Journal of a Tour to the Hebrides with Samuel Johnson* P. 143.
25 Flora MacDonald's letter to John MacKenzie, (NLS shelfmark: MS. 1306, f. 72)
26 Ibid
27 Flora MacDonald's letter to Sir John MacPherson, (shelfmark: MS 2618, ff 82–84)
28 Douglas, Hugh. *Flora Macdonald, The Most Loyal Rebel*, p. 214.

Robert Bontine Cunninghame Graham.
From an original print c.1920.

Robert Bontine
Cunninghame Graham

R OBERT Bontine Cunninghame Graham was born into a
Scottish aristocratic family on 24th May 1852 in London.
He grew up in the family estate of Gartmore in Perthshire, but also
spent many of his early years on the family estate of Finlaystone
in Renfrewshire. He was the eldest of three sons of Major William
Cunninghame Bontine and Anne Elizabeth Elphinstone Fleeming.[1]

In his early years, he spent much of his time in the care of his
Spanish-born grandmother, who passed to him her knowledge of
Spanish culture and language.

Privately educated until the age of 14, he attended his first formal school at Hill House in Leamington Spa in England where his
Aunt Helen, who kept horses, taught him to ride before being sent
to Harrow boarding school.

His mother owned a literary salon in London, frequented by
many of the greatest writers and personalities of the generation.
Cunninghame Graham, from an early age, met, mixed with, and
befriended many of those who were to become household names,
authors Neil Munro, Joseph Conrad, Henry James, Oscar Wilde
and George Bernard Shaw, to name only a few.

His father, who had suffered a blow to his head while serving as
an officer in Ireland, became increasingly violent and depressive,
resulting in the family seeking specialist care for him in a facility
in Dumfriesshire. His illness and his inability to run the estates
were ruinous, resulting in Cunninghame Graham having to leave
Harrow. Leaving the constraints of Harrow proved to be fortuitous
as, after a spell of private tuition in London, he was sent to the

Consular Chaplain in Brussels who ran a school and taught, among other things, languages and fencing.

His great niece, Jean Cunninghame Graham, or Lady Polwarth as she is known, says of her great-uncle, "*He loathed public school with its bullying and snobbery and was extremely glad when family finances forced his withdrawal*". Perhaps this was the catalyst that encouraged the 17-year-old to seek a life of adventure. On his own, he set off for Argentina, intending to make his fortune and restore the family honour. Lady Polwarth writes, "*He was always incredibly happy on the back of a horse, so South America was right up his street*".

Family contacts arranged a position for Cunninghame Graham with a cattle ranch in Argentina and, shortly after, he found himself on a ship heading for South America. Within two weeks of arriving, he discovered that the two Scots he was supposed to partner were alcoholics. Alone, he talked his way into being accepted by a group of cattle drovers on a cross-country trip. At first, as he could speak the language so well, they suspected he was not a foreigner, but his skills on a horse were superior to many men and he won them over.

Within days, the group met a band of men from the Revolutionary Army in Uruguay, which led to Cunninghame Graham's conscription. Again, his fellow soldiers refused to believe he was a foreigner. They decided that he must be pretending, but as he was a willing rebel, he was accepted. Far from being alarmed by his predicament, he loved their way of life. Living on horseback, travelling over the Pampas plains seemed an ideal way to live. Robert settled into life as a gaucho so completely that they parted as friends.

Argentina offered an adventurous life but his many enterprises, including cattle droving and horse trading, all failed to provide a regular income, leading to his return to Britain in his early twenties. His time in South America may have been a financial failure, but the experience shaped his thinking and moral outlook for the years to come.

His life as a gaucho earned him the title of 'the Gaucho Laird', or, as he became known throughout South America, 'Don Roberto'. His experiences of living and working with the poorest of people, treated appallingly by uncaring landlords and politicians, never left him, influencing his political views and forming the inspiration for his collection of short stories.

When he was 26, he met the 19-year-old Gabriela de la Balmondiere, in Paris. Many accounts of his life tell that they met when the pair collided on horseback; however, Lady Polwarth explains that they simply met in a park. It was a perfect match, a meeting of souls. Both spoke several languages, loved to travel, and both became successful authors. Gabriela would go on to become a campaigner for women's rights, a water-colour painter, botanist, mystic, and the author of several well-regarded books. They married in South America just months after meeting.[2]

After their wedding, Robert and Gabriela moved to Texas, where they set up a ranch. They became close friends of Buffalo Bill Cody, who they met when Cody was making the first of his travelling 'cowboy' shows at Horsehead Crossing, near to the Mexican border. A short time later, they moved to Mexico, travelling on a wagon train from San Antonio, where he taught fencing.

In 1881, a Native American war party burned the ranch to the ground and drove off all their cattle, prompting an early return to Britain. Despite this, Robert offered his full support to the cause of the Native Americans.

When Robert was in his mid-30s, Keir Hardie, urged him to stand for Westminster. On his travels, Cunninghame Graham had seen for himself, and supported the plights and causes of the poor and downtrodden, from the treatment of the Native Americans, to the abandoned and neglected people of Argentina, to the poor and hungry of Great Britain. Hardie said that Parliament wasn't ready for "... *me with my cloth cap yet*", but they would look at Cunninghame Graham as one of their own and listen to his ideas.

In the 1886 general election he was selected as the Liberal Member of Parliament for the North Lanarkshire constituency, but it soon became obvious that his ideas were far from those held by any previous Liberal MP. He called for the abolition of the House of Lords, denounced capitalism, imperialism, called on help for the unemployed, an eight-hour day for workers, free school meals, and home rule for Scotland.

He regularly came into conflict with the Speaker. On one occasion, he was asked to retract an accusation against a fellow MP, famously replying, "*I never withdraw!*" This led to a suspension from Parliament. [3] On another occasion, he became the first MP to be suspended for swearing in the House of Commons when he made a 'disrespectful reference' by using the word 'damn' during a speech.[4]

On the 13th November 1887, Cunninghame Graham was arrested for his part in a riot in Trafalgar Square.[5] Along with fellow member, Labour MP John Burns, they were charged with "*Unlawfully and riotously assembling together to the terror of Her Majesty's subjects*", with a further charge of assaulting the police. The following day, when they appeared at the Bow Street Police Court, Cunninghame Graham's head was "*... extensively bandaged*".

Cunninghame Graham had intended to speak at the rally in support of Irish home rule; however, on November 8th, five days before the event, the Commissioner of Police, sanctioned by the Home Secretary, issued a notice prohibiting meetings in Trafalgar Square. They claimed, regardless of any previous use of Crown property, there was no right for persons to go there to make speeches, or to attract persons to listen to speeches. When the marchers, who numbered several hundred, approached Trafalgar Square, at the forefront were Cunninghame Graham and Burns who found that police had deployed themselves around the Square, effectively blocking any access.

It was at this point that Cunninghame Graham and Burns rushed across the road arm in arm and tried to break through the police ranks. In the ensuing struggle, the police, armed with truncheons, claimed the men threw punches. Both men were arrested and charged.

On 21st November 1887, the Scottish Miners National Federation agreed to support a proposal to be made at their National Conference, calling on miners to work a five-day week and eight hours daily. A motion was also agreed that if Cunninghame Graham was imprisoned *"… the working classes in the country should so claim a national strike until he was released"*.[6]

At the conclusion of the trial at the Central Criminal Court on 18th January 1888, the jury consulted for 35 minutes before finding Cunninghame Graham and Burns guilty of unlawful assembly, but acquitted the pair on charges of riot and assault. Both defendants were sentenced to six weeks' imprisonment, without hard labour, which was served in Pentonville Prison, London.[7]

Gabriela, replying to a letter of sympathy from Lanarkshire miners, confessed that she received letters of the most *"fearful description"* from men of society. She explained that it was comforting *"… for a woman in distress who was persecuted by "gentlemen" to receive the affectionate sympathy of 30,000 miners."*[8]

Cunninghame Graham continued to court publicity by stating his intention to appear in the House of Commons, when they debated the Trafalgar Square question, wearing a facsimile of his prison suit.[9] It is reported that, while in prison, he had a portrait photograph taken of himself, posing in his prison outfit, and distributed it as his

R. B. CUNNINGHAME GRAHAM ON "LUCERO," CARTAGENA DE INDIAS.

R. B. Cunninghame Graham on Lucero.
From Cartagena and the Banks of the Sinú.
by R. B. Cunninghame Graham.
Published by William Heinemann. London. 1922.

official photograph as Deputy Lieutenant of the County of Stirling. Four weeks later, on the 18th February, both men were released to be greeted by a crowd of supporters, including Gabriela and his mother and brother. They made their way to London, where, the same evening, a meeting of sympathisers filled the Craven Hall in Regent Street. Both Cunninghame Graham and Gabriela spoke to the enthusiastic crowd.[10]

He fought for Scottish Home Rule to have the "*... particular pleasure of knowing that the taxes were wasted in Edinburgh, instead of London*". Soon after Trafalgar Square, he became the first president of Scottish Labour when he formed the Independent Scottish Labour Party with Keir Hardie, who became secretary.

In March 1889, in the Commons, he was challenged to answer whether he championed the cause of 'pure unmitigated socialism'. Cunninghame Graham replied "*Undoubtedly*", confirming himself as the first socialist elected to Parliament.[11]

Around 1890, on a visit to Glasgow, Cunninghame Graham saw a horse rearing up while the operators were trying to attach the harness to allow it to pull a tram car. He managed to calm the animal and, so impressed was he by the horse, contacted the Glasgow Corporation and bought it, an Argentine stallion. Of all the horses he had owned, it became his favourite. He called it Pampa and rode it for the following 20 years.[12]

Still passionate about his many causes, in 1891 he travelled to France as a guest speaker at a socialist meeting. At the end of the evening, he was asked to meet the local police commissioner, who was waiting in an adjoining room. The moment he entered, he was placed under arrest and served with a warrant ordering his immediate expulsion from France. He was taken from the hotel and deposited on the English mail boat leaving at 1.30am for Dover. A French newspaper, ironically titled *La Liberté*, noted, "*We can only congratulate the Government on the expulsion of M. Cunninghame Graham. ... While M. Cunninghame is endeavouring to relieve French workmen, his wife is running all over Spain making Socialist speeches, which have a great success, rather like that of a Spanish farce".*[13]

For the 1892 general election, Cunninghame Graham was nominated for the Glasgow Camlachie seat. A meeting held to ratify and select a candidate, held in the Campbellfield Street Hall on 20th May, developed into a riotous affair with competing factions all but coming to blows in support of their own man. At the end of a prolonged evening, where several policemen attended to ensure the meeting passed peacefully, Cunninghame Graham stood as the nominee, gaining 185 votes for, and 85 against.[14]

Cunninghame Graham, in the end standing as an Independent Scottish Labour Party candidate for Glasgow Camlachie, lost the vote, ending his parliamentary career. Keir Hardie was elected as a Labour MP.

George Bernard Shaw told of a day when walking in London with his mother, they passed the immaculately dressed Cunninghame Graham in the street. Acknowledging each other as they crossed paths, Bernard Shaw told his mother that the man was Cunninghame Graham. The old lady replied, *"Nonsense. Cunninghame Graham is one of your Socialists; that man is a gentlemen."*[15]

This perception that he could not be a socialist because of his dress and status in life may have swayed the people of Glasgow Camlachie in choosing not to re-elect him. Certainly, there were elements within the Labour Party who resented what they saw as his 'grandstanding' in parliament. *The Labour Leader*, a party newspaper of the day, wrote in 1908, *"The suggestion that Labour members, because they are Labour members, should play the part of rowdies in Parliament is essentially a snobbish one. It springs from the idea that working-men are by nature noisy and undisciplined, that a democrat*

PORTRAIT OF THE AUTHOR AS SHEIKH MOHAMMED EL FASI

R. B. Cunninghame Graham in disguise
as Sheik Mohammed El Fasi.
From his book, Mogreb-El-Acksa,
A Journey in Morocco.
Published by the New York,
National Travel Club. 1930.

must be a demagogue, ... and Mr. Cunninghame Graham reserves all his turbulence for violent words on socialist platforms while he leads a scrupulously law-abiding life among the exploiters of the poor in the West End of London".[16]

However, other elements of the Scottish political arena thought differently. When Cunninghame Graham once more attacked the government for expressly refusing to consider taking part in discussion of the eight-hour working day at the Berne International Convention on Labour in Factories, a daily newspaper commented, *"... if he has not the finesse and subtlety of an old parliamentary hand, he has, at any rate, the courage of his convictions, and will fearlessly attack questions that have proved far too tough for solutions to all previous comers in the arena of reform".* Continuing, *"... he forces matters to the front in their boldness, that have long badly needed definite solution, but which by reason of their perplexing character, have been evaded by the more cautious of the regular party rank and file on either side of the house".*

With the end of his parliamentary career, he and Gabriela took to travelling, writing and adventure. They journeyed to Spain in 1894 in an unsuccessful search for a lost gold mine.

Then on to Morocco where he disguised himself as a Turkish sheikh to try to enter Tarondant, a city forbidden to outsiders. Reuter's Tangier correspondent reported the account by Cunninghame Graham: *"Full of hope and expectation we left Mogador on the 12th October (1897)."* Their first setback occurred shortly after the entrance to the Imine Tan'aut Pass where they were informed that it would be impossible to proceed safely, forcing a detour on a track which would take much longer. *"... late in the afternoon, and no-one was to be seen, when suddenly from somewhere or other a number of people came running towards us shouting and wildly gesticulating. I did not like the look of things very much. ... however, an old man stepped forward and offered us a bowl of corn and milk, for which we thanked him and offered to pay. He said he did not want money, only the holy man's blessing. ... It was not until the interpreter reminded me that I was disguised as a Sherief, that I understood what was expected of me, so I mumbled a few words of no particular language which the translator conveyed to the old man. We were blessed by him in return and continued our journey, very glad to have escaped so cheaply".*[17]

All continued well, until they were about eight hours' ride from Tarondant, when they found themselves surrounded by a body of armed mountaineers. Cunninghame Graham added, "*... it was evident by their signs that we were to go back, and if we refused, their only too eloquent dumb show gave us to understand we should be killed where we stood. It was no use in resisting, we were escorted back about eight miles. ... We were packed in a small tent with our muleteers and baggage, where we remained for ten weary days. The answer from the court came to the effect that we were to return. ... We lost no time in loading our mules, and made our way to Marrakesh by forced marches, thence we reached the coast, and got back to Tangier".*[18]

In his 40s, he began to write. While in South America he would regularly write long narrative letters to his mother, and his books became an extension of these letters, leading to his first book of short stories, published in 1895. He published 40 books in all, at a rate of almost one a year. Today, Cunninghame Graham is looked upon by many as the finest short story writer this country has ever produced.[19]

In September 1906, the couple were travelling to Spain when Gabriela died suddenly at the small French town of Hendaye in the Pyrenees. Some reports mention that she had been ill for some time, but nevertheless, her death was completely unexpected.[20]

She was buried in the ruins of the 13th century monastery on Inchmahome Island in the Lake of Menteith, the ancient resting place of the Lairds of Gartmore. It was reported that, "*Beyond a small circle in London and the tenantry of Gartmore. Mrs Cunninghame Graham was little known. She was the daughter of Don Francisco José de la Balmondiere, and her sympathies were largely Spanish.*"

After 28 years together, such was Robert's devotion to his beloved Gabriela that, with an assistant, he dug her grave himself.[21]

At her funeral service, the coffin was borne to the old landing stage and placed on a small boat that carried Gabriela to her final resting place. Her death was devastating for Cunninghame Graham; he never remarried, and visited her grave regularly for the remainder of his life.

In January 1910, the Aberdeen Socialist Club contacted Cunninghame Graham asking him to run as a socialist candidate for South Aberdeen. He replied by telegram, noting that he had no great desire to *"re-enter the national gaswork".[22]*

For the final years of his life, he devoted himself to Scottish self-government. He became the president of the Scottish Home Rule Association from the early 1920s before, in 1928, he became the president of the National Party of Scotland. This then united with other nationalist parties, creating the Scottish National Party in 1934, with Cunninghame Graham acting as president from its foundation.[23]

On 1st June 1929, Cunninghame Graham was the guest of honour at a Glasgow dinner of the Scottish PEN Club, a group *"committed to fostering a dynamic literary culture in Scotland",* and *"... champions a freedom of expression and literature across borders".* Cunninghame Graham, a founder member, in replying to suggestions that he might better have devoted his talents entirely to Scottish literature, pointed out that the Scottish and Spanish temperaments were extremely alike, with a pawky humour equally evident in both Spanish and Scottish writers. They had another, more modern, similarity: a strong home rule movement in Catalonia corresponded largely to the Scottish National movement – which unfortunately had received a slight check – but was *"... undoubtedly going to be the greatest movement in the country".[24]*

He was a firm believer not only in independence for Scotland but also acted as an advocate of home rule for the other countries of the United Kingdom. He never laid blame or harboured any animosity against the English, famously saying, "*The enemies of Scottish nationalism are not the English. Our real enemies are those among us born without imagination*".

He travelled through Columbia and Brazil, where he wrote his book, *A Brazilian Mystic*. Whilst in Paraguay, he travelled on horseback 600 miles up the river Parana to the Iguaçu Falls to visit desolate Jesuit ruins. His research and record of Spanish brutality against the native people became his acclaimed book *A Vanished Arcadia* – which became the Oscar winning feature film *The Mission* in 1986.[25]

In 1936, age 84, already suffering ill health, and against the wishes of his doctor, he visited Argentina, knowing it would be for the last time. Robert Bontine Cunninghame Graham died in the Plaza Hotel, Buenos Aries of pneumonia, on 23rd March 1936.[26]

A fulsome obituary appeared in the later editions of *The Scotsman* in the afternoon of his death.[27]

His body lay in state at the Chapelle Ardente, where the President of the Argentine Republic paid a personal visit to make his country's condolences. Over the following 24 hours, a constant stream of members of the public filed respectfully past his remains. Thousands of people lined the streets of Buenos Aires as the funeral cortege made the short journey to the *Almeda Star* to begin his voyage home to Scotland, via Plymouth.[28] Two horses followed the funeral cortege, Cunninghame Graham's boots reversed in the stirrups.[29]

On board the Blue Star liner, tributes were paid by the British Ambassador and the President of the Academy of Letters, who presented a wreath of flowers sent by the Argentine Government.[30]

As a sign of respect, the Uruguayan Government arranged for a

The Funeral of Mr R B Cunninghame Graham.
"The coffin was taken across to the Isle of Inchmahome in the
Lake of Menteith, where the burial took place."
From an original copy of The Times. April 1936.
© Jerry Brannigan

wreath of flowers to be placed on his coffin as the ship sailed past Montevideo.[31]

On the morning of 18th April, on the same day as his funeral in Scotland, a memorial service took place at St Michael's, Chester Square, London.[32]

In the afternoon, his funeral service took place in Perthshire, in the small local church adjacent to the Lake of Menteith, crowded with villagers, farmers and many representatives from the worlds of literature, art, and politics.[33]

A piper then preceded six mourners who carried the casket to a small launch for the final part of the journey to Inchmahome Island where he was to lie alongside his beloved Gabriela in the ancient grounds of Inchmahome Priory.[34]

In 1986 Gabriela's true identity was made known. She had run away from home to become an actress, resulting in her exclusion from her family in Marsham, Yorkshire. Her real name was Caroline (Carrie) Stansfield Horsefall, daughter of a surgeon. Robert knew her secret, but that only made her more attractive. To the rest of the world, she was a half French, half Chilean poet. It is thought that, with the collusion of his mother, the three created a new identity for Carrie, ensuring her acceptance into their society. It is not known how many members of the family knew; regardless, they were sworn to secrecy, a secrecy they kept long after her death.

In Argentina, Cunninghame Graham was long regarded as a national hero, known as 'Don Roberto' and the 'Father of the Gaucho'. Through his short stories, he brought the world of the South American gaucho, and life of the ordinary people, to the outside world.

In Buenos Aires there is a street, Roberto Cunninghame Graham, named in his honour. A village named after him, Don Roberto, lies in the province of Entre Rios, close to the border with Uruguay.[35]

In April 1936, it was reported that Cunninghame Graham had bequeathed many of his personal possessions and paintings to the Smith Institute. The Cunninghame Graham Library was opened in the Stirling Smith Art Gallery and Museum in 2016 and is the only library facility in the UK dedicated to the life and work of Cunninghame Graham.[36]

On Saturday 27th June 1936, shortly after his death, on the anniversary of the Battle of Bannockburn, his chair, draped with the Graham tartan, was left vacant at the demonstration in Kings Park in Stirling. As honorary president, he had never missed a Bannockburn anniversary.[37]

The Cunninghame Graham Memorial is a monument dedicated to the memory of 'Don Roberto' Robert Bontine Cunninghame Graham (1852–1936) 15th of Gartmore and 19th of Ardoch. The monument was built the year following his death, consisting mainly of Scottish stones but also including stones from Argentina, Uruguay and Paraguay. Originally situated at Castlehill, Dumbarton, it was moved in the 1970s to the village of Gartmore, where until 1900, Gartmore House had been the principal seat of the Cunninghame Graham family.[38]

Below an inset medallion his epitaph read:

Robert Bontine Cunninghame Graham
Famous Author, Traveller and Horseman
Patriotic Scot and Citizen of the world
A Master of life, A King Among Men.

References

1   Spartacus Educational. *Robert Cunninghame Graham.* https://spartacus-educational.com/TUcunninghame.htm
2   Cosimo Books, *R.B. Cunninghame Graham.* http://cosimobooks.com/classics_author.php?author=3424
3   *Yorkshire Gazette,* 8th December 1888, p. 11. col. 4.
4   *St Andrews Citizen,* 7th May 1892, p. 8. col. 1.
5   *The Watford Observer,* 21st January 1888, p.3. col. 2.
6   *South Wales Daily News,* 22nd November 1887, p. 3. col. 5.
7   *Aberdeen Press and Journal,* 19th January 1888, p. 4. col. 1.
8   *South Wales Echo,* 15th February 1888, p. 4. col. 7.
9   *South Wales Echo,* 16th February 1888, p. 3. col. 1.
10 *Otley News and West Riding Observer,* 24th February 1888, p. 6. col.1.
11 *Spartacus Educational.* Robert Cunninghame Graham.
12 Bottle Imp, *Cunninghame Graham: Scotland's Forgotten Writer,* p. 7.
13 *Exeter Flying Post,* 16th May 1891, p. 7. col. 4.

14 *Glasgow Evening Post*, 20th May 1891, p. 2. col. 4.

15 *Hartlepool Northern Daily Mail*, 23rd March 1936, p. 4. col. 2.

16 *Labour Leader*, 8th May 1908, p. 9. col. 1.

17 *St James's Gazette*, 23rd November 1897, p. 6. col. 2.

18 *Westminster Gazette*, 11th November 1897, p. 5 col. 3.

19 Bottle Imp, *Cunninghame Graham: Scotland's Forgotten Writer*, p. 4.

20 *Dundee Courier*, 12 September 1906, p. 4. col. 6.

21 *Coatbridge Leader*, 22nd September 1906, p. 6 col. 4.

22 *Dundee Courier*, 6th January 1910, p. 4. col. 4.

23 *The Scotsman*, 23rd May 1934, p. 11. col. 5.

24 *The Scotsman*, 3rd June 1929, p. 7. col. 2.

25 Aimé Tschiffely, *Long Rider*. www.aimetschiffely.org/rbcg.htm

26 *Liverpool Echo*, 21st March 1936, p. 3. col. 4–5.

27 *The Scotsman*, 23rd March 1936, p. 10. col. 3–4.

28 *The Scotsman*, 17th April 1936, p. 8 col. 7.

29 *The Scotsman*, 24th March 1937, p. 15. col. 4.

30 *Dundee Evening Telegraph*, 27th March 1936, p. 15. col. 4.

31 *Hartlepool Northern Daily Mail*, 26th March 1936, p. 6. col. 7.

32 *Dundee Evening Telegraph*, 15th April 1936, p. 5. col 7.

33 *Linlithgowshire Gazette*, 24th April 1986, p. 3. col. 6.

34 *Dundee Evening Telegraph*, 17th April 1936, p. 10. col. 6.

35 *Aberdeen Press and Journal*, 11th August 1941, p. 2. col. 6.

36 *The Scotsman*, 21st April 1936, p.11. col. 4.

37 *The Scotsman*, 26th June 1936, p, 12. col. 4.

38 *The Scotsman*, 14th June 1937, p. 16. col 4.

The Capture of Isabella, Countess of Buchan.
An original illustration by Lancelot Speed (1860–1931)
The Days of Bruce by Grace Aguilar. 1880.

Isabella, Countess of Buchan

ISABELLA Macduff was born around 1286, the second child of Duncan Macduff, 7th Earl of Fife and Lady Joan de Clare. Her elder brother Duncan later became a ward of Edward I.

As a teenager, she was married to John Comyn, 3rd Earl of Buchan, a nobleman and head of one of the most powerful families in Scotland, who was around 35 years older than his countess. Arranged marriages were commonplace amongst the political elite, designed to create bonds between powerful families and for the continuance of heirs to estates and titles. The legal age for a girl to marry in Scotland in 1300 was 12 years old (14 years old for a boy) with the girl having no say or rights in the matter, often meeting her husband for the first time at the wedding ceremony.

John Comyn's cousin and namesake, known as the Red Comyn, was a bitter rival of Bruce for the Scottish throne. When Robert Bruce ran a dagger through his heart, it set in motion a series of events that would have huge repercussions throughout Scotland and change Isabella's life for the worst.

Bruce played a long political game. At one stage, to maintain his position with Edward I, he became part of the fight against William Wallace. It is likely because of this considered approach he was made joint Guardian of Scotland with the Red Comyn. In forcing the two to work together, Edward knew it would weaken not only Bruce and the Red Comyn's support, it would also damage their claims to the Scottish throne.[1]

In 1304 Robert the Bruce's father died. This was a pivotal time for Bruce, giving him, in his eyes, a stronger claim to the Scottish Crown. On 10th February 1306, Bruce met the Red Comyn at Greyfriars Kirk in Dumfries. The meeting did not go well. Previous encounters had ended in acrimony and blows and, as discussion once again became heated, Bruce plunged a dagger into Comyn's heart. According to legend, when Bruce told his men he thought he had killed the Red Comyn, Bruce's men returned to the church, with Roger Kirkpatrick reporting back to Bruce that he had '*mak sicc*'. He made sure.[2]

He may not have planned to murder Comyn, but Bruce knew that to commit murder in front of the altar of Greyfriars Kirk meant excommunication once news reached Rome. As an excommunicated man, he could never be king; Bruce had to act swiftly.[3] He immediately went to Robert Wishart, Bishop of Glasgow, who absolved him of his sin, thereby allowing plans to be made for Bruce to be crowned as quickly as possible. It was Wishart who had the coronation robes and banners hidden in his treasury[4] and, before Pope Clement V or Edward I could act on the news, Bruce headed to Scone Abbey, the traditional crowning place of Scottish kings. In the absence of the Stone of Destiny, it was essential that this ceremony be carried out in as much of the traditional setting and manner as possible.[5]

By custom, the Earls of Fife claimed a hereditary right to place the crown on each new monarch's head, and next in line to carry out the family tradition was Countess Isabella's brother, Duncan. Having been taken to England, as a ward of Edward, the secrecy around the coronation meant Duncan could not be considered.

On the 25th March 1306, Robert the Bruce was crowned King Robert I by William Lamberton, Bishop of St Andrews, in the presence of the Bishops of Glasgow and Moray, alongside the Earls of Atholl, Lennox, Menteith and Mar.

It is not known how the countess heard of the coronation – possibly from a trusted member of her household – but regardless of how she came to know, as a MacDuff, Isabella had a profound sense of family tradition. It would have been a heart-searching, agonising decision for the 19-year-old to make, especially as she knew there would be severe repercussions. Aware that her husband and his family

King Robert I.
Robert the Bruce, King of Scots.
Stirling Castle.
© *Jerry Brannigan.*

were loyal to Edward and would look upon this as an act of treason, she still had an unflinching sense of moral duty to take her brother's place, for her family honour, and for Scotland. Undeterred, she took off with her husband's best horses, and headed to Scone.[6]

Hours after the coronation by Lamberton, 19-year-old Isabella MacDuff, Countess of Buchan, arrived to claim her family right to crown Scotland's king.

Bruce realised that a crowning by a MacDuff would lend legitimacy to his reign and, in his desperation to ensure his coronation be seen to follow the rites of ancient tradition, 48 hours later the ceremony was restaged. This time Isabella MacDuff, Countess of Buchan, laid the circlet of gold on the head of Robert Bruce. He was now Robert Bruce I, King of Scots.[7]

When news of the coronation reached Edward, he was apoplectic with rage, immediately mobilising his troops for a swift and merciless reprisal. Bruce, aware that he would be hopelessly outnumbered, charged his brother Neil to take the ladies of the Scottish court to Kildrummy Castle in Aberdeenshire for their safety. The party numbered his Queen Elizabeth and young daughter Marjorie, along with his two sisters Mary and Christina. Countess Isabella, although not a member of the Scottish royal family, had nowhere to turn; her husband had issued her death warrant for her treachery, leaving her no option but to join the ladies in their flight.

Bruce had taken refuge in Argyle when news reached him that the Earl of Pembroke waited in Aberdeen for the arrival of additional troops led by Edward's son. Bruce sent word to his brother to move the ladies from Kildrummy Castle.

As the English army laid siege to Kildrummy, Sir Neil Bruce remained behind with the garrison to defend the castle for as long as possible, giving the women time to escape. It was reported that Neil Bruce suffered a betrayal when the castle blacksmith started a large fire making defence impossible. When the garrison did eventually capitulate, every man was executed. In legend, it is said that the black-smith's reward was in gold, molten, and poured down his throat. Sir Neil Bruce was captured and taken to Berwick, where he was hanged, drawn and beheaded.[8]

The royal ladies, with the countess, were almost certainly trying to escape to Orkney. There they would find a boat to take them to safety in Norway where Bruce's sister was queen consort to King Eric II. The women made it only as far as St Duthac's shrine in Tain, where they were betrayed by the Earl William of Ross and captured by Edward's men.[9]

John of Strathbogie, Earl of Atholl, who escorted the women, was taken to London and hanged. Edward heeded a plea for mercy in consideration of John's high status as an earl in typically brutal fashion, ordering his gallows be 30 feet higher than normal to signify his status. His body was burnt, and his head displayed on London Bridge on a pole taller than those unfortunates whose heads were also displayed around him. No earl had been executed for 230 years.[10]

For the ladies of the Scottish Court, a series of humiliating punishments were conceived.

Elizabeth, Bruce's queen, was the daughter of Richard, 2nd Earl of Ulster, an important ally of Edward, and her treatment reflected this. Elizabeth was placed under house arrest in the manor of Burstwick-in-Holderness and allowed two ladies-in-waiting, with the particular specification that they should be elderly and *"not at all gay"*.

Christina Bruce, whose husband Sir Christopher Seton had been recently hanged, drawn and quartered, was sent to a convent in Sixhills, Lincolnshire, to be imprisoned in one room for the duration of her captivity.

For Bruce's 12-year-old daughter Marjorie, Bruce's sister Mary and Countess Isabella, Edward ordered they be kept in *"Kages"*.

The first order deemed that Marjorie, still a child, be treated with 'great severity'. She was originally sentenced to be held in a cage in

The Countess of Buchan's Cage.
As described by the instructions of King Edward I.
© David Alexander.

the Tower of London; later, Edward revoked this order, sending her instead to a nunnery at Walton, Yorkshire.[11]

Lady Mary and Countess Isabella were both sentenced to be imprisoned in cages 'strengthened with timber and iron'.

For Lady Mary, whose husband Sir Neil Campbell still fought with Bruce, he ordered that she be locked in a wooden cage to be built jutting from the battlements at Roxburgh Castle. However, in February 1311, Lady Mary was released in a prisoner exchange.[12]

Feb. 8. The K. commands the sheriff of Northumberland to deliver Mary de Brus, a Scottish prisoner in Newcastle-on-Tyne, to Philip de Moubray, to exchange her for his brother Richard de Moubray, a prisoner with the Scots.[13]

The order for Countess Isabella's punishment was explicit: "*... that she should be placed in a cage in one of the turrets of Berwick Castle, of strong lattice work of wood, and well strengthened with iron: and she is to be so safely kept in such cage, that she can in no wise come out of the same. The Chamberlain is to assign or appoint one or two women of said town of Berwick, English, and free from suspicion; ... she may not speak to any man or woman of the Scottish nation, nor, indeed, to anyone else, excepting the women so appointed*".[14]

In a further pronouncement, Edward I ordered: "*Let her be hung up out of doors in the open air at Berwick, that in life and after her death, she may be a spectacle and eternal reproach to travellers*".[15]

The instructions set out by Edward mention they should be set inside, which may mean the cages were on the inside perimeter of the castle, or within a room, which may have been the case for Mary. However, the tone of Edward's order leaves no doubt that he wanted to make an example of Isabella. One writer of the day likened the cage to "*A little house of timber, the sides latticed so that all could gaze on her*".

As a non-royal, Isabella was subjected to the harshest treatment. Edward I, also known as 'the Hammer of the Scots', could not treat these women as brutally as he had treated the captured men, the majority of whom he had executed in a horrific variety of ways. These women either had political or family connections which had to be respected, or more likely, as members of Bruce's family, would have great hostage value. Care had to be taken that they did not die in his custody.

Isabella dying in custody was not such a worry. Her actions at the coronation demonstrated the greatest disrespect, not only to her husband John Comyn, but to her king, which he took personally. It was Edward's view that as she made the choice to be there, making a public spectacle of her was a much more satisfying outcome.

In the following months and years, Bruce took to the country and mountains.[16] Over time, his small army, using guerrilla tactics, won many skirmishes with the English, culminating in a stunning victory at Bannockburn in 1314. This was the turning point. The capture of almost 100 English earls and knights, all of them valuable hostages, meant that Bruce now had the bargaining tools to finally bring home the ladies of the Scottish Court.[17]

He wasted no time in discussing terms for the return of the ladies. *The Calendar of Documents Relating to Scotland of 1890*, chronicles orders from the King: "*July 18th 1314, The King commands the Prior of Sixhills to deliver Christiana sister of Robert de Brus, widow of Christopher de Seton, to the sheriff of Lincoln to be brought to him at York*".[18]

Lady Christina Bruce was released from her imprisonment shortly after Bannockburn. She continued to play an important part in Scottish politics until her death in 1357, at the age of 84.

"*October 2 1314, the King sends Robert Bishop of Glasgow, the Countess of Carrick wife of Robert de Brus, with his sister and daughter and Donald de Mar, to Carlisle Castle, to be taken thence to a place arranged by the Earl of Essex and Hereford and the sheriff of York*".[19]

Five months after Bannockburn, Elizabeth was freed at Carlisle and returned to Scotland. Marjorie was released from her solitary confinement into the care of Walter Stuart, 6th High Steward of Scotland, who had distinguished himself at Bannockburn. Bruce rewarded him with Marjorie's hand in marriage. Two years later, on 2nd March 1316, while riding in the grounds of Gallowhill, Paisley, a heavily pregnant Marjorie was thrown from her horse. Seriously injured, she went into premature labour, and was delivered of a son by caesarean section in nearby Paisley Abbey.

Marjorie died shortly afterwards. The child, her only son, survived and in 1371, succeeded his uncle David II of Scotland as Robert II, King of Scots.

Mary Bruce endured four years in her cage. After her exchange, she returned to Scotland and married twice.

Elizabeth, Marjorie, Christina and Mary all left captivity and resumed their lives. The Countess of Buchan remained in her cage for nearly four years, a spectacle for all to look upon 24 hours a day, 365 days a year. She was treated like an animal in a zoo until, in 1310, Edward II allowed her to be taken to the House of the Carmelites at Berwick. She appears to have been imprisoned there until, on "*April 28th 1313, Edward commanded his warden of Berwick-on-Tweed and constable of the castle to deliver Isabella, widow of John Earl Buchan, a prisoner there since the late king's time, to Henry de Beaumont.*"[20]

Henry de Beaumont was one of the 'disinherited', meaning he had fought against Bruce and had therefore forfeited all his lands. Through his marriage to Alice Comyn, de Beaumont claimed the Comyn title and became the 4th Earl of Buchan. For many years thereafter, he urged Edward III to challenge for the Scottish crown and return a Balliol to the throne. Finally, in 1335, Sir Andrew Moray ruthlessly defeated the invaders at the Battle of Culblean, causing Henry de Beaumont to flee back to England, where he lived the remaining period of his life. When he died in 1340, his son refused the earldom, ending the Comyn lineage.[21]

Countess in a Cage.
An original illustration by Lancelot Speed (1860–1931)
The Days of Bruce by Grace Aguilar. 1880.

Isabella, Countess of Buchan

It is deeply ironic that Isabella was released into the care of Henry de Beaumont and Alice Comyn, her niece by marriage to John Comyn, the man who signed her death warrant. There are no records concerning Isabella MacDuff, Countess of Buchan, after she was handed over to them.

References

1 Weeks, Lyman Horace, *Book of Bruce, Ancestors and Descendants,* p. 79.
2 Ibid
3 Oram, Richard, *Kings and Queens of Scotland,* Tempus, Stroud, 2006, p. 120.
4 Oram, Richard, *Kings and Queens of Scotland,* p. 121.
5 Weeks, Lyman Horace: *Book of Bruce, Ancestors and Descendants,* p. 80.
6 Tranter, Nigel, *The Story of Scotland,* Wilson, Glasgow, 1987, p. 67.
7 Weeks, Lyman Horace, *Book of Bruce,* p. 81.
8 Cornell, David, Bannockburn, The Triumph of Robert the Bruce, 2009, Yale University Press, p. 63.
9 Tranter, Nigel, The Story of Scotland, Wilson, Glasgow, 1987, p. 67.
10 Cornell, David, Bannockburn, 2009, p. 65.
11 Cornell, David, Bannockburn, 2009, p. 66.
12 Cornell, David, Bannockburn, 2009, p. 65.
13 Bain, Joseph, *Calendar of Documents Relating to Scotland,* Volume Three, Ref. Feb. 8. 1311. 244.
14 Francis Palgrave, *Documents and Records relating to the History of Scotland. 1837. P. 354.*
15 Tain District Museum, *The Treaty of Auldearn, 1308.* https://www.tainmuseum.org.uk/articles.php
16 Oram, Richard, *Kings and Queens of Scotland,* p. 123.
17 Oram, Richard, *Kings and Queens of Scotland,* p. 125.
18 Paris, Matthew, *Calendar of Documents Relating to Scotland,* 1890, Ref. Oct 2. 1314. 256.
19 Bain, Joseph, *Calendar of Documents Relating to Scotland,* Volumes One to Four. London, p. 74.
20 Bain, Joseph, *Calendar of Documents Relating to Scotland,* Volume Three, Ref. April. 28. 1313. 313.
21 Bain, Joseph, *Calendar of Documents Relating to Scotland,* Volume Three, Ref. Dec. 12. 1312. 296.

Acknowledgements

Alan Fletcher

Alan's name was suggested to me by my nephew's wife, Claire, with a trail leading very quickly to Alasdair Gray. We had met previously, we had friends in common, and I had his email address. He replied within the hour with his telephone number asking me to call "... whenever you like." Whenever I liked was 10 minutes later, and after a long conversation, Alasdair's love, respect and admiration for his Glasgow School of Art companion was as evident then as it must have been almost 70 years earlier when they first met.

It was a pleasure to meet Alasdair and talk about Alan. That Alasdair died before Alan's story saw publication was a blow, but I am pleased he knew that his friend's life and work would not be forgotten.

It was lovely to meet and chat to Hannah and Ronnie McCorkindale. Hannah is Alan's niece, who recalled the many happy days of her youth mixing with her uncle and his painting pals. I have to thank both Hannah and Ronnie for their generosity in allowing me into their home to examine the Alan Fletcher-related material they have looked after for so long, and of course, for the many cups of tea.

I was so pleased to meet Carole Gibbons in her beloved Kelvingrove Art Gallery and Museum over a coffee, and again at her exhibition, *From the Studio Winter Show*, at the House for an Art Lover. Many thanks to Carole and her son, Henry Guy, for assistance and permissions.

I also have to thank Sorcha Dallas Gray and all at the Alasdair Gray Archive for their assistance and enthusiasm for my Alan

Fletcher project, and for Sorcha's desire to create an Alan Fletcher archive, which would bring Alan's life and work into the overall care of the Alasdair Gray Archive.

Thanks also to Jennifer Lightbody and staff at the Archives and Collections Department of the Glasgow School of Art, who gathered related documents which were sorted and waiting at my appointed time.

Thanks to Jayne Stewart, Collections Manager at the Hunterian, University of Glasgow, and all staff at the University of Glasgow Special Collections.

Thank you also to Lili Bartholomew, Museum Registrar at The McManus: Dundee's Art Gallery and Museum, for arranging my access to the Alan Fletcher work in the archive and for permissions.

Victoria Drummond

With thanks to Catherine Drummond-Herdman for the invitation to visit the family at Megginch Castle, and to examine memorabilia, photographs, and Victoria's dress uniform.

Thanks to Martin Byrne, Federal Secretary of the Australasian Institute of Marine Engineers for his assistance.

It was also very thoughtful of Sister Thomas, Chair of Trustees, Augustinian Care, St

George's Park, Ditchling Common, Burgess Hill, not only to speedily answer a query that had arisen, but who also recalled that she looked after Ms Drummond in her final days and remembered her well.

James Finlayson

Many thanks to Fanny Badoc for her English/French and French/English translation skills, which leads to thanks to Monsieur Combier of Images et Loisirs/Monsièur Cinema for permission to use their cart fiches.

Beatrice Clugston

I have to thank Peter McCormack (retired) Museums Development Officer, East Dunbartonshire Leisure & Culture Trust for his assistance and enthusiasm in my efforts to highlight Beatrice's life to a wider audience and for arranging permissions for images supplied.

I must also thank both Emma Sunter and Gillian Kealey, Local Studies Officers, for their assistance, in particular for inviting me to talk on Beatrice Clugston as part of East Dunbartonshire's Local History Month in March 2023.

I would also like to thank Scott Crawford author of The History of Broomhill and Lanfine Homes for his enthusiasm and assistance.

Thanks to Deborah Carmichael of Kirkintilloch Rotary and Jenny Burgon of the Soroptimists International of Kirkintilloch for guiding me through the many people and groups involved in the restoration of the Beatrice Clugston Monument, and for their efforts in safeguarding Beatrices memory in the housing development of Broomhill Estate.

Dr John Rae

Many thanks to Mark Newton, Trustee of The John Rae Society and Andrew Appleby, President, for their support and use of photographs.

Rose Reilly

I had known about the exploits of Rose Reilly since she was inducted to the Scottish Football Hall of Fame and had always earmarked her as a potential subject should this book see publication. Therefore, it was a very happy coincidence that with our move from Glasgow to Stewarton I was to see Rose regularly around her home town. Many thanks to Rose for her assistance.

Thanks to Margot McCuaig of Purple TV for her advice and images.

Thanks also to Susie Van der Post, Commercial & Events, Professional Footballers' Association Scotland.

Ben and George Parsonage

I have to thank George Parsonage for welcoming me into his home, and garden, to chat about his truly remarkable life. Having spent the first 10 years of my own life living close to Glasgow Green and the River Clyde, I already knew a little of the history of the Parsonages and the Glasgow Humane Society.

It has been a great honour to meet and get to know George: being in his company, listening to his recollection and experiences, makes my life seem less significant each time we meet.

Many thanks for the use of family-related documents and photographs, with permissions as stated.

Mary Mitchell Slessor

I have to thank Douglas Binnie, Chair of the Mary Slessor Foundation, for giving me a personal walking tour of Dundee, highlighting the important places in Mary's life. Also, for supplying images and permission to use others.

Thank you also to Lili Bartholomew, Museum Registrar, The McManus: Dundee's Art Gallery and Museum.

Acknowledgements

Alexander Grant

Thanks to Anna Hawkins, Museum Collections Manager, Centre for Research Collections, The University of Edinburgh Main Library for supplying a high-resolution image and permission to use the portrait, 'Sir Alexander Grant' by Sir William Samuel Henry Llewellyn. (EU0942)

Many thanks to Philip Wright, The Media Centre, Pladis Global, London, for permission to use a portrait of Sir Alexander Grant from the Pladis archives. https://www.pladisglobal.com

Flora MacDonald

Thanks to the Ashmolean Picture Library, Ashmolean Museum, University of Oxford, for advice regarding the Flora McDonald Portrait by Alan Ramsay.

Special thanks to illustrator David Alexander for his eye-catching drawings featured in the biographies of Victoria Drummond, James Finlayson, John Rae, and Isabella, Countess of Buchan.

THIS book wouldn't have happened without the assistance of two groups of people.

Firstly, many thanks those who nominated subjects: Heather Anderson, Claire Cameron, Arnie Faichnie, Tony Green, Dr Helen Marlborough, Linda Duncan McLaughlan, Margaret McLellan, Sheila Penson, Susan Stewart, and Garry Waltham.

Secondly, to my group of beta readers, from those who read one biography to those who read all twelve. Your feedback was invaluable, challenging, and thought provoking. Your work is very much appreciated.

Bibliography

Alan Fletcher
Schotz, B, *Bronze in my Blood: The Memoirs of Benno Schotz* (Edinburgh, 1981).
Glass, Rodge, *Alasdair Gray: A Secretary's Biography* (London, 2008).
Gray, Alasdair, *A Life in Pictures* (Edinburgh, 2010).
Hardie, William, *Scottish Painting 1837 to the Present* (3rd edn, Glasgow, 2010).

Victoria Drummond
Drummond, Cherry, *The Remarkable Life of Victoria Drummond: Marine Engineer* (London, 1994).
MacCarthy, Fiona, *Last Curtsey: The End of the Debutantes* (London, 2006).

James Finlayson
Amalgamated Press, *Film Fun Annual 1939* (London, 1939).
Louvish, Simon, *Stan and Ollie: The Roots of Comedy; The Double Life of Laurel and Hardy* (London, 2002).
MacKinnon, Murray, and Oram, Richard, *The Scots: A Photohistory* (New York, 2003).

Beatrice Clugston
Hillhouse, Robert, *Bygone Years of the West of Scotland Convalescent Seaside Homes*, Dunoon (Glasgow, c.1909).

John Rae
McGoogan, Ken, *Fatal Passage* (n.p.2001).

Bibliography

Mary Slessor

Kumm, H.K.W., *African Missionary Heroes and Heroines* (New York, 1917).

Livingstone, W.P., *Mary Slessor of Calabar: Pioneer Missionary* (London, 1926).

Enock, Esther E., *The Missionary Heroine of Calabar: A Story of Mary Slessor* (London, 1937).

Ben and George Parsonage

Shields, John, *Clyde Built: A History of Shipbuilding on the River Clyde* (Glasgow. 1949).

Parsonage, George, *Rescue is his Business, The Clyde His Life: The Story of Ben Parsonage & The Glasgow Humane Society* (Glasgow, 1990).

Herman, Arthur, *The Scottish Enlightenment: The Scots Invention of the Modern World* (London, 2003).

Alexander Grant

Hessell-Tiltman, H., *James Ramsay MacDonald: Labour's Man of Destiny* (London, 1929).

Flora MacDonald

Boswell, James, *The Journal of a Tour to the Hebrides with Samuel Johnson, LLD* (London, 1773; facs, edn, NLS. DNC23 1852).

Mackenzie, Alexander, *The Life of Flora MacDonald and Her Adventures With Prince Charles* (Inverness, 1882, facs, edn NLS Shelfmark A110 e) p. 116.

Jolly, William, *Flora MacDonald in Uist: A Study of the Heroine in Her Native Surroundings* (Perth, 1886).

Forbes, Robert, *The Lyon in Mourning*, Vol I (1895, rep, edn (NLS shelfmark SCS. SHS. 20-SCS. SHS. 22).

MacGregor, Alexander, *The Life of Flora MacDonald* (Stirling, 1901).
Craig, Maggie, *Damn' Rebel Bitches: The Women of the '45* (Edinburgh, 1997).
Douglas, Hugh, *Flora MacDonald: The Most Loyal Rebel* (n.p.2003).

Robert Bontine Cunninghame Graham
Cunninghame Graham, R. B., *Cartagena and the Banks of the Sinú* (London, 1922).
Cunninghame Graham, R. B., *Mogreb-El-Acksa* (New York, 1930).

Isabella, Countess of Buchan
Palgrave, Francis, ed., *Documents and Records Illustrating the History of Scotland, and Transaction Between the Crown of Scotland and England,* Vol I (n.p.1837).
Aguilar, Grace, *The Days of Bruce* (London, 1852).
Paris, Matthew, ed., Flores Historiarum, *Calendar of Documents Relating to the History of Scotland,* Vol III 1200–1259, Vol V (1108–1516). Published 1890.
Weeks, Lyman Horace, *The Book of Bruce, Ancestors and Descendants of King Robert the Bruce of Scotland* (New York, 1909).
Scott, Ronald McNair, *Robert the Bruce: King of Scots* (n.p.1996).
Tranter, Nigel, *The Story of Scotland* (Glasgow, 2001).
Oram, Richard, ed., *Kings and Queens of Scotland* (Stroud, 2006).
Cornell, David, *Bannockburn: The Triumph of Robert the Bruce* (London, 2009).